Knitted Lace of ESTONIA

TECHNIQUES, PATTERNS, *and* TRADITIONS

NANCY BUSH

INTERWEAVE
interweavebooks.com

Editor Ann Budd
Technical Editor Lori Gayle

Cover Design | **Art Direction** Pamela Norman
Interior Design Mark Lewis
Illustration Gayle Ford

Photography Joe Coca
Technical Photography Ann Swanson

Interweave Press LLC
201 East Fourth Street
Loveland, CO 80537-5655
interweavebooks.com

Printed in China by Asia Pacific Offset

Library of Congress
Cataloging-in-Publication Data

Bush, Nancy, 1951-
  Knitted lace of Estonia : techniques, patterns, and
traditions / Nancy Bush,
author.
    p. cm.
  Includes index.
  ISBN 978-1-59668-053-1 (pbk.)
  1. Knitted lace--Estonia--Patterns. 2. knitted lace-
-Estonia--Haapsalu. I.
Title.
  TT805.K54B84 2008
  746.2'26028094798--dc22

                    2008008684

10 9 8 7 6 5 4 3 2

For the Knitters of Haapsalu

Writing this book has been an extraordinary journey. My understanding of this knitting tradition could not have been accomplished without help from many generous people.

My first Estonian lace lesson came from Hilja Aavik, teacher and friend since the beginning of my Estonian experience. I visited Haapsalu the first time with Anu and Ulla Kaljurand. They are my Estonian "family" and helped in so many ways as I worked on this project. Laila Põdra and her parents, Avo and Aino, have also welcomed me, offering encouragement, friendship, and translations.

In Haapsalu, I had help, instruction, memorable afternoons, and cherished friendship from Linda Elgas, Silvi Sarlo, Miralda Piper, Laine Põldme, Aime Edasi, and Aime Saareleht. Aide Leit-Lepmets, while not a knitter, learned a lot about knitting while translating and answering many e-mails with "very odd" questions. Eve Otstavel and Asta Veenpere at Haapsalu's Läänemaa Muuseum have shared photographs and information about the history of these shawls.

Ellen Värv, my friend at the Estonian National Museum in Tartu gave me access to their collection of shawls, photographs, and documents.

My friend Maret Tamjärv and I visited Milvi Heli, a third-generation Haapsalu lace knitter. Maret translated while Miliv told about knitting lace. Milvi gave me the lilac-wood knitting needles, shown on page 11, made by her great uncle.

Leili Reimann welcomed me to her home and answered many questions about Estonian lace, Madli Puhvel and Rita Tubalkain translated the editions of Leili's books for me. Juta Kurman gave permission to reprint patterns from *Haapsalu Rätik,* and Helena Soomer translated the text for me.

My friends Ene and Alar Sokk have been on this journey with me almost from the beginning. Ene traveled with me to Haapsalu and translated my first lessons about their shawls. She shared her collection of Triinu, which opened up a whole world of Estonian lace patterns and is a wonderful addition to this research. Aire Salmre and Helle-Mall Risti added information about Triinu and gave encouragement and translation help. Helgi Leesment wrote an article for the North American Estonian newspaper about my research. As a result, I contacted Maria Ormerod and her mother, Helve Poska, one of the original lace pattern contributors to Triinu. Maria translated her mother's story for me. Also, Leida Pukk and Helve Arro sent me shawls knitted by their mothers. These are treasures they have shared.

I had help knitting the shawls from Melanie Elizondo and Marge Yee–Norrander. Vonnie Wildfoerster and Patrick de Freitas read texts, made suggestions, and kept me on task.

Editor Ann Budd made working on this book a delight. I value her advice and friendship. Lori Gayle's thoughtful, careful technical editing assures that knitters will be able to reproduce the projects. Joe Coca's photographs bring the projects to life. Many folks at Interweave—Tricia Waddell, Rebecca Campbell, Gayle Ford, Ann Swanson, Nancy Arndt, Pamela Norman, and Mark Lewis—contributed to the creation of this book.

I've saved this spot for Joe Gardner, my husband, and Mac, our furry housemate. They have been patient and supportive, and I promise I'll have more time for walks now.

I thank all of you for your patience, kindness, friendship, and love.

—*Nancy*

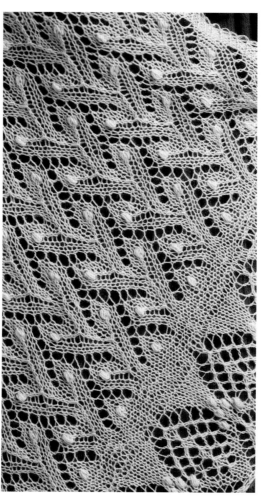

TABLE OF CONTENTS

INTRODUCTION

I discovered the lace knitting from Haapsalu on my first visit to Estonia in 1995. On that trip, I found several handknitted shawls, including one with patterns resembling sprigs of Lily of the Valley, which I brought home as a gift for my mother. As I looked at these marvelous knitted items, originally purchased as gifts, not for research, I became curious about their origins and the special techniques involved.

When I began to ask questions, I was told about the town of Haapsalu on the west coast of Estonia, and how these shawls were connected with the history of the town. Although it began as a cottage industry rather than a folk tradition, the lace knitting of Haapsalu and Estonia in general has become a cherished tradition in its own right.

To learn more, I visited Haapsalu, to breathe the sea air, walk the lanes between the wooden houses, and stroll along the promenade where the knitters sold their wares. I wanted to understand the Haapsalu of 100 years ago, as well as the Haapsalu of today. One of the knitters in Haapsalu told me; "if you visit Haapsalu and see smoke coming from the chimney of a house, there will be a woman inside, knitting lace." I love the image of a woman knitting by the fire, keeping a tradition alive that began nearly 200 years ago.

I have traveled to Estonia many times in recent years and have had the honor and delight to spend considerable time with the knitters in Haapsalu as well as in Tallinn, who keep this tradition alive. They have made me tea, offered me cake, and tried to answer every conceivable question—mostly through animated "international acceptable body language." I have had a taste of learning "knee to knee" from the masters of this craft.

Haapsalu knitter Maria Bogdanova with shawl on blocking boards, 1950s. Photo courtesy of Läänemaa Muuseum, Haapsalu.

Although I originally thought that there was a single "right" way to knit these shawls, I have learned that there are nearly as many "ways" as there are knitters. Just like handwriting, each knitter has her own way of knitting certain parts of a shawl, and I found that it is quite acceptable to make a change because it worked better for me. I have tried to emphasize the few hard and fast rules that there are.

My desire for this book is to tell the story of Haapsalu lace knitting and to record some of the patterns that are part of this story. I've stayed true to traditions I learned from the knitters of Estonia in the patterns for the shawls and scarves included in this book. But, just like my handwriting, they reflect my personality. For example, I used yarn that is available on my side of the world and by doing so, my shawls and scarves have a different look than the ones I have carefully collected and studied. I also chose to use yarns for a few of the projects from fibers not common to Estonian knitters, like qiviut (fiber from the musk ox) and cashmere. Every knitter needs a bit of luxury. That being said, I mostly chose 100% wool, as wool is what the Estonians typically use. I believe these patterns respond best to wool.

This has been a wonderful adventure and it is my pleasure to share it with knitters everywhere.

THE LACE KNITTING
of HAAPSALU

Knitters in Haapsalu, from left to right:
A. Amberg, H. Lao, I. Tammik, L. Tamberg,
A. Klems, K. Kõrv. Date and photog-
rapher unknown. Photo courtesy of
Läänemaa Muuseum, Haapsalu.

Located along the Baltic coast, Estonia neighbors Latvia to the south, Russia to the east, and Finland to the north (across the Finnish Sea). Estonia has a long history of knitting and is home to some

Estonia neighbors Latvia to the south, Russia to the east, and Finland to the north.

of the oldest knitted artifacts in Northern Europe, dating from the end of the thirteenth century. Knitting, particularly of mittens, gloves, and socks, has played a major role in Estonia's customs and traditions for hundreds of years.

On the west coast of Estonia is the resort town of Haapsalu, famous for its thirteenth-century castle ruins, curative mud baths, and pleasant beaches. Haapsalu was a small settlement in the thirteenth century when it became the seat of power for the ruling Bishops of Western Estonia and the nearby islands. The town grew around the castle complex, including a fortress and cathedral, which date from around 1280.

Three hundred years later the last bishop sold the territory to the Danes and the subsequent years saw various rulers, as all of Estonia was subject to invasion and warfare. During the seventeenth century Estonia enjoyed relative peace under Swedish rule. Many of the islands and parts of western Estonia had been settled by Swedes as early as the thirteenth century, and Haapsalu served as the unofficial capitol for Swedish Estonians. Even today, the people of Haapsalu and surrounding areas look to Sweden with respect.

Russia ruled Estonia from the early eighteenth century until 1918. It was during this period that Haapsalu became a destination for tourists and a flourishing resort town. The women of Haapsalu, being industrious and creative, began a cottage industry of knitting lace shawls that has continued into the twenty-first century.

Many countries have long-standing traditions of lace or openwork knitting. Two well-known traditions are Shetland lace from the North Sea islands northeast of the Scottish mainland and Orenburg lace from the southern tip of the Ural Mountains in central Russia. The Orenburg tradition traces its origins to the second half of the eighteenth century and records of the Shetland tradition date after 1830.

Most Haapsalu lace patterns are created on a stockinette-stitch ground. Shetland lace, in contrast, is usually worked on a garter ground, though sometimes a stockinette-stitch ground is used. Orenburg lace patterns are generally worked on a garter-stitch ground. The Estonian lace patterns can be classified as "lace knitting"; knitted fabric that has a row of plain knitting (or purling) after every pattern row—the pattern is worked on right-side rows only. "Knitted lace," by contrast, is knitted fabric in which the pattern is worked on every (both right side and wrong side) row. Shetland and Orenburg patterns contain examples of both.

THE BEGINNING OF A TRADITION

While no definitive historic data exists, it is believed that the tradition of lace knitting in Haapsalu began in the early nineteenth century, at about the same time that Haapsalu became a popular summertime destination for wealthy Russians, Germans, Swedes, and other Europeans. The lure of Haapsalu was largely due to restorative mud baths. The first sanatorium

Three generations of knitters, from left to right: Juuli-Marie Kesker (1894–1966), Hirlanda Kesker (1913–1992), and Milvi Heli (1937–). Photographer unknown. Photo courtesy of Milvi Heli.

was opened in 1825, the second in 1845. These baths attracted many tourists, who came by boat and train to enjoy the spas and the picturesque town. Haapsalu became a favorite destination for St. Petersburg royalty, including Tsar Nicholas I (1796–1855) and Alexander II (1818–1881). Haapsalu gained royal status with these visits and enjoyed a summer social "season."

The tourists, whose numbers reached close to 3,000 at the end of the nineteenth century, were undoubtedly dressed in the finest fashions, which possibly included delicate knitted lace shawls and scarves. It is likely that these fashions inspired experienced Haapsalu knitters to develop lacy patterns of their own. Tradition has it that the skill of knitting these shawls may have come with a family from Noarootsi, the Swedish-speaking peninsula just across the bay north of Haapsalu, when they settled in Haapsalu.

No matter how the idea began, the knitters in Haapsalu created a cottage industry at which they excelled. The knitters would gather on the promenade, a popular walkway along the shoreline in the town, sitting in groups with their baskets of shawls, their knitting in their hands, listening to music from the bandstand and selling their wares to wealthy tourists. Many vacationers bought Haapsalu shawls to take home as gifts, and soon the shawls became well known throughout Europe and the Nordic countries. Knitters also congregated at the seaport where ships would stop on their way from Riga, Latvia to Tallinn to St. Petersburg. Many bulk purchases of "theater shawls" were bought by Russians and sold to the wealthy St. Petersburg

ladies. The shawls from Haapsalu were at the height of their popularity at the end of the nineteenth century and the beginning of the twentieth century.

An accomplished knitter could complete twenty to thirty shawls during the quiet winter months; a family working together could complete as many as seventy or eighty shawls for the high season. Girls were taught to knit "knee to knee" at an early age by their mothers. They were taught simple patterns when they were as young as four years old, and by the time they were eight, they could be trusted to knit the lace edgings that were sewn onto the completed centers. There were generations of knitters in these families; mothers who taught their daughters who in turn taught their own daughters the patterns and technical details of making these shawls. Even young boys helped with the knitting, albeit they were reluctant to have others know about it.

The Estonians had no written instructions for their patterns—the techniques and designs were handed down from one generation to the next. Stitch patterns were preserved on long knitted samplers or on individual sample pieces. The knitter would study the sample and decipher the pattern without the aid of

Sampler of lace patterns knitted in Haapsalu. The needles, a precious gift from Milvi Heili, were handmade by her great uncle. Photo by Ann Swanson. Sampler knitted by Miralda Piper.

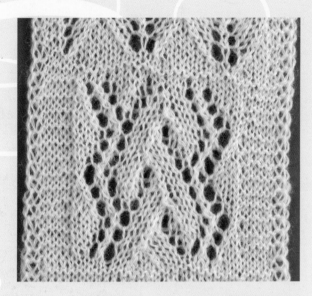

Detail of a twig pattern in the sampler knitted by Miralda Piper. Photo by Ann Swanson.

charts or written instructions. If a knitter borrowed a sampler to learn a new stitch pattern, the loan was repaid with a new pattern added on to the sampler. It wasn't until the 1930s that printed patterns with graphed symbols were used.

In the nineteenth century there were only a few patterns such as *haga* (twig), *lehe* (leaf), and *raha* (money). Since then, tens of dozens of patterns have been developed, many of which reflect everyday life and the Estonian deep involvement, respect, and love for nature. Some of these are *liblikakiri* (butterfly pattern), *mustikakiri* (blueberry pattern), *kaselehekiri* (birch leaf pattern), and the beloved *maikell* (lily of the valley) pattern. The maikell pattern and its many variations,

as well as numerous other patterns, incorporate the textured technique called *nupp* (knob or button— rhymes with soup). This bobble-like feature is a specialty of Estonian lace knitting and is used to add texture in openwork patterns or to create a figure or image on a stockinette-stitch ground. Shawls were typically sold by weight, and those containing nupud (nupps) weighed more and could bring a higher price. Nupps were (and still are) proof that a shawl was handknitted, as they cannot be made by machine.

The early styles of shawls from Haapsalu were made from relatively thick singles or two-ply handspun wool from local sheep. Although the soil around Haapsalu was poor, sheep survived on the grass between juniper trees. The best wool for these shawls was from the back and neck areas of young sheep. Thick yarns were spun on a spindle, but the best yarn for knitting lace was spun on a wheel. Fine yarn was desirable, and mill-spun yarn, often imported, was popular when it became available.

The early shawls were simple without an *äärepits* or *pits* (the lacy scalloped edge). Later, as fine mill-spun yarn became available, the shawls grew airier and more complicated with the addition of a scalloped edge. It is said the finest shawl could pass through a wedding ring, the age-old measure of quality of this type of knitting. This fineness was coveted as an attraction for prospective buyers. The most popular color was and still is white. Some shawls were knitted with pastel shades, while those knitted out of gray or black yarn were typically reserved for local use.

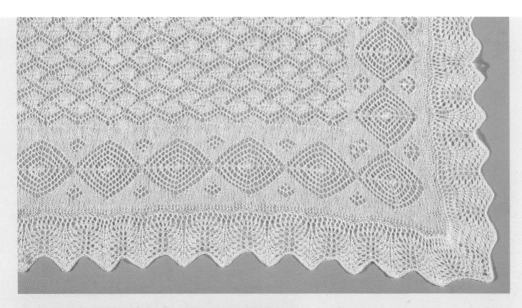

Above: Detail of square shawl knitted by Linda Elgas. Left: Rectangular shawl from the craft cooperative UKU. Photos courtesy of Estonian National Museum.

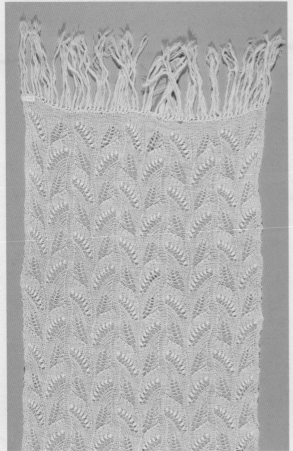

Traditionally, the knitters used single-point needles that were hand-carved from lilac or apple wood, both common in local gardens. The needles were sanded, then oiled with sheep's wool. They were made in sizes ranging from about U.S. size 2 or 3 (2.75 or 3.25 mm) up to U.S. size 6 (4 mm). Needle size was determined by measuring the width of the hole made when a needle was punched through a piece of paper. The needles were short, measuring around 10" (25 cm) long and were smooth and lightweight, with rounded—not sharp—points. Today's knitters continue to prefer short, smooth, lightweight commercial wood or bamboo needles; they never use metal needles, which they consider too heavy. The knitters in Haapsalu typically carry their yarn in their right hand and "throw" the yarn in the "English" method of knitting.

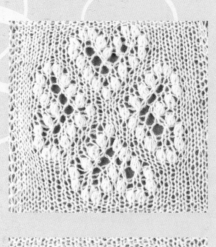

Top to bottom:
Greta Garbo
motif, Crown
Prince motif, and
Queen Silvia
motif. Photos by
Ann Swarnson

THE TRADITIONAL SHAWL

The classic Haapsalu shawl, popular at the end of the nineteenth century and the beginning of the twentieth century, was square, measuring about 40" × 40" (100 × 100 cm) or larger and consisted of three distinct patterns—one for the center, another for the border, and a third for the edging. The center and border were knitted in one piece and although both included openwork designs, it was only the edging that was called "lace." Traditionally, the edging was knitted separately in two parts and sewn onto the main piece. The edge was worked in two parts (often with more than 250 stitches in each) because half of the edging stitches would fit on the short, single-point needles, which were also used for the center and border. The knitters did not use circular (which are a modern invention) or double-pointed needles for their shawls.

Square shawls were typically folded in half and worn over the head so that the lace edging framed the face. If a hat was worn in the winter months, the shawl was placed over the top of the hat. By the 1930s, machine-spun yarn was used and rectangular shawls or scarves decorated with long fringe were common, as were smaller rectangles (with or without the lace edging) and triangular scarves. These rectangular shawls or scarves were and still are made with just a center section and an attached edge; there is no border design between the two.

Anette Martson (left) and her sister Anna Kütt (center) meet with a prospective buyer in Haapsalu, 1963. Photographer unknown. Photo courtesy of Läänemaa Muuseum, Haapsalu.

In addition to motifs based on nature, accomplished knitters also developed designs to honor famous people. A shawl made with the Greta Garbo (1905–1990) motif, a design that incorporates hearts, was sent to the film star in 1935 in hopes that the "divine" Garbo would wear it in one of her films and bring recognition to Haapsalu. A shawl made with the *kroonprintsi*, Crown Prince motif, was given to the Crown Prince of Sweden, Gustav Adolf (1882–1973) upon his visit to Haapsalu in 1932. The Crown Prince motif was adapted from the *Muhu mand* pattern ("Muhu twirling stick of pine" or "Muhu Pine," an eight-pointed star pattern used on traditional clothing from the island of Muhu) on an antique knitted mitten. The original Crown Prince pattern was designed by Matilde Möll, who was one of the first to graph the stitch patterns for Haapsalu lace and possibly one of the first to knit triangular shawls. More recently, Linda Elgas, an honored knitter in Haapsalu, designed a beautiful pattern incorporating the *liblikas* (butterfly) and *maikelluke* (lily of the valley) patterns. A shawl in this new pattern, slightly reworked, was given to Swedish Queen Silvia (1943–) when she visited Haapsalu in 1992 and as a result, was named the Queen Silvia pattern.

THE TRADITION CONTINUES

During Estonia's first independence (from 1920 to 1940), knitting courses were taught at the local technical college in order to organize and encourage knitters in Haapsalu. This is where teachers were trained and students could take courses in the special techniques involved in Haapsalu shawls. This period saw recognition of Haapsalu shawls, which were advertised worldwide in the 1930s. Also during this time, many Estonian knitters took part in international exhibitions as far away as Berlin and New York.

One master knitter, Anette Martson, (born 1879) had more than fifty knitters working for her, to whom she distributed yarn. She finished the knitted shawls by washing and blocking them and she organized their sales. In the 1930s, more than 500 residents of Haapsalu were involved in knitting shawls. Anette Martson's shawls were in numerous exhibitions and she received many awards for her work.

Tariffs imposed in the early 1930s inhibited the importation of fine knitting yarn from Sweden, England, and Latvia, and some knitters moved abroad to Latvia

and Finland in order to continue their work. Others started knitting sweaters with openwork patterns as a substitute for the shawls. A business, *Kodukäsitöö* (Home Handicraft) was started in 1927 that exported knitted goods to Europe and the United States.

World War II disrupted the Estonian export industry, but during the Soviet occupation from 1944 to 1991, the knitters of Haapsalu carried on knitting shawls and scarves. Shawls and scarves were produced through the craft cooperative, UKU, which operated a workshop in Haapsalu. Each participating knitter had to complete a quota of nine shawls or twelve scarves each month. Older knitters with disabilities were given half that quota. UKU provided the yarn to the knitters, who were paid very little for their work.

In the 1970s, the director of UKU in Haapsalu, Leili Leht, began collecting, recording, and photographing patterns for shawls and scarves. According to Linda Elgas, in her book *Haapsalu Rätikud*, this collection formed the basis for three editions of Leili Reimann's book *Pitsilised Koekirjad*. Reimann is not a native of Haapsalu, but her book made many of the patterns that originated in Haapsalu available to knitters throughout Estonia and beyond.

PRINTED PATTERNS

During the war years, many Estonians fled to Sweden, Canada, Australia, and the United States. Although these refugees had few worldly possessions, the women brought their knitting skills and traditions with them. In an effort to protect and preserve na-

TRIINU

Triinu magazine was the idea of Vera Poska-Grünthal, a graduate of Tartu University and lawyer. She, along with three other Estonian women; Aede Kivilo-Gold, Linda Rõõmusmägi-Pahk, and Elsa Kesskküla, all living in Swe-

den after the war, founded *Triinu* in 1952. These women were experts in Estonian national costume, handicrafts, and cuisine, and understood the need for a magazine to keep their traditions alive and to connect their fellow Estonians dispersed throughout the world. As the only Estonian language publication, *Triinu* united Estonians around the globe, fostering a sense of national pride and enriching their lives with Estonian traditions by providing a means to maintain contact with their language and customs.

The magazine was published quarterly, one for each season. Vera Poska-Grünthal remained editor in chief until her death in 1986. At that time, her daughter, Tanni Kents, who was living in Toronto, took over the editorship until the last issue in 1995. By that time 171 issues had been published.

In the 1960s, Poska-Grünthal organized a series of co-editors who shared the responsibilities of publication on a rotating basis. The spring issue was organized by the editors in Australia, summer was handled in Sweden, autumn in the United States, and winter in Canada. The editors and contributors were volunteers who found time to work on the magazine between their regular jobs and family responsibilities. They were motivated by a sense of nationalist pride and good will, and they never received monetary compensation.

Early copies of the magazine were simple copied pages of type. As the magazine grew, it was printed with color and on finer paper, with striking covers, often depicting nature, crafts, or textiles. There was an inspirational message at the beginning of every issue. Pages to follow contained poetry, articles on literature, art, culture, health, nutrition, and recipes. Each issue also featured a photograph of a young woman in regional national costume along with patterns and instructions for making the depicted items.

Leili Leht, Director of UKU in Haapsalu, organized shawl and scarf production during Soviet occupation. Photographer unknown. Photo courtesy of Läänemaa Muuseum, Haapsalu.

tional customs and the traditions of Estonia, especially among children growing up away from their homeland, *Triinu* magazine (see sidebar on page 17), the only Estonian language home and family magazine, began publication in the autumn of 1952. In addition to articles about culture, arts, cuisine, and events, many issues included patterns for knitted mittens, hats, and especially shawls and scarves, in the Haapsalu tradition. It isn't possible to overemphasize the importance this magazine had in promoting and preserving Estonian handicrafts and applied arts among Estonians living and growing up abroad.

Another source for shawl patterns was the book *Haapsalu Rätik*, published in 1972 by the Federated Estonian Woman's Clubs in New York. This publication offered some history of the craft, written (not graphed) patterns for centers, borders, and edges, and a pattern for a triangular shawl. The information was compiled by displaced Estonian knitters, some who had learned their skills in Haapsalu before the war, in order to connect to other Estonian women cut off from their homeland. Both *Triinu* and *Haapsalu Rätik* allowed Estonian knitters worldwide to learn about and practice their traditions.

TODAY

Today there is a flourishing market for the lace shawls of Haapsalu, in the town itself as well as shops in Tallinn and elsewhere in Estonia. The knitters in Haapsalu still make their shawls in the traditional method, with the lace edge, if there is one, attached by sewing it to the completed center. While some square shawls are still knitted, most are now rectangular. Triangular shawls are also popular.

Lacy knitting for making shawls and scarves has spread to other parts of Estonia. Examples from various villages are among the collection at the Estonian National Museum. While the patterns and techniques may not be the same as those developed in Haapsalu, there are many similarities. Today in Estonia, the title *Haapsalu rätik*—Haapsalu shawl—refers to any knitted lacy shawl or scarf, regardless of where in Estonia it was knitted or if it is a square, rectangle, or triangle. All are recognized as part of an honored Estonian tradition.

Leili Leht inspects
a shawl for UKU.
Photographer unknown.
Photo courtesy of
Läänemaa Muuseum,
Haapsalu.

HOW *to* KNIT *a* HAAPSALU SALL

The term *Haapsalu rätik* (Haapsalu shawl or scarf) seems to be a universal title for a lace shawl or scarf in Estonia. In Estonia, a true Haapsalu rätik is square, while a triangular shawl is known as a *kolmnurk rätik* and rectangular shawls or scarves are known as *sall*. All are made with openwork lace patterns, whether traditional or newly designed, and if there is an *äärepits* or lacy edge for a traditional style, it is always knitted separately and sewn to the completed center section by hand. A newer, nontraditional style of construction is to pick up and knit the lace edge onto the completed shawl center. Instructions are given here for both methods. There is much more to these shawls than meets the eye. It is the small details that make them so interesting and fun to knit.

CENTER SECTION

To design a rectangular sall (shawl or stole), begin by choosing a stitch pattern for the center section from the stitch dictionary on pages 122–145. See pages 24–27 for instruction for knitting nupps and special stitches used in many of the patterns. Knit a sample swatch of the pattern, perhaps two repeats wide and two repeats high, then bind off the stitches. Block the swatch to open up the lace design. When dry, measure the width and height. Use these measurements to determine the number of pattern repeats you'll want for the shawl center, which will determine the number of stitches to cast on. Be sure to add balancing stitches if necessary to make the pattern match or create a mirror image at the two selvedge edges. When deciding on the number of pattern repeats, keep in mind that blocking will add considerable length and width, as will the addition of frame stitches and a lacy edge. The average size for a finished rectangular shawl from Haapsalu measures about 23½" (60 cm) wide and 67" (170 cm) long.

BEGINNING FRAME

The center section is always surrounded by a narrow garter-stitch frame. If a lace edge will be attached, the frame is usually eight rows (four garter ridges) tall at the top and bottom and four stitches wide along each side. If there will be no lace edge, the garter frame is usually five garter ridges tall at the top and bottom and five stitches wide along the sides. The frame at the bottom and top of the shawl must complement

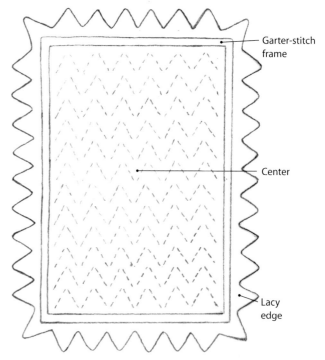

A Haapsalu *sall* consists of a center section bordered on all sides with a frame and lacy edge.

the frame at each side. When planning your own design, be sure to add in these frame stitches to the total stitch count for the width and row count for the length.

Using the elastic knitted method (see page 23), cast-on the desired number of stitches. Except for the very first row after the cast-on, begin every row with a slipped stitch (the first stitch of the first row is

KNITTED LACE OF ESTONIA

CAST-ON AND EDGE STITCHES

KNITTED CAST-ON

In Estonia, this cast-on is called *veniv kootud serv* or stretchy knitted cast-on. Make a slipknot and place it onto the left-hand needle. Bring the right-hand needle into the slipknot as if to knit, wrap the yarn around the needle (Figure 1), and pull through a new stitch. Place this new stitch onto the left needle, in front (to the right) of the slipknot (Figure 2). Repeat from *, always inserting the right-hand needle into the last stitch formed. Cast on with the yarn doubled if casting on for a lacy edge (cast on with a single strand if casting on for the center section). At the end of the cast-on row, break one end and continue for the rest of the edge with a single strand. Often there are two knitted rows worked directly after the doubled cast-on before the pattern stitch begins.

EDGE STITCHES

To ensure a tidy edge for picking up into later, the first stitch of every row should be slipped purlwise. I like to knit the first stitch of the very first row—right after casting on—because the first stitch has little support. After the first row, I slip all of the edge stitches. To slip this edge stitch, hold the yarn in front, slip the first stitch as to purl (Figure 1), then place the working yarn to the back, between the slipped stitch and the next stitch so the yarn is in the position to knit (Figure 2), and continue across the row as usual. This will cause the edge stitches to be slightly twisted.

There are two exceptions to this rule. One exception is the triangular shawl in which stitches are cast on for the two side edges and the shawl is worked to the center of the top edge, decreasing stitches along the way. In this case, the edge stitches are worked into the decreases instead of being slipped. The other exception is garter-stitch lace edges that will be sewn onto the shawl center. These edge stitches are knitted, not slipped.

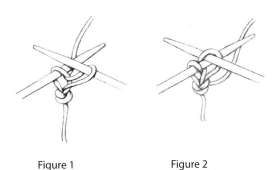

Figure 1   Figure 2

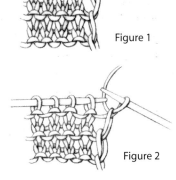

Figure 1

Figure 2

knitted) to form a selvedge edge (see page 23) that is easy to see when sewing on or picking up and knitting the lace edge later. Slip this edge stitch purlwise with the yarn in front, then return the yarn to the back between the two needles in preparation to knit the next stitch.

CENTER PATTERN

Work your chosen number of garter rows, then beginning with a right-side row, work the center pattern. To help keep track of the garter-stitch frame at each side, place markers after the frame stitches on the right edge (as seen when the right side is facing) and before the frame stitches on the left edge. Repeat your chosen center pattern for the desired number of pattern repeats.

ENDING FRAME

Work eight or ten rows (four or five garter ridges) of garter stitch to mirror the garter frame rows worked at the beginning of the piece and end having worked a right-side row.

With the wrong side facing, use the k2tog bind-off (see page 27) to bind off all of the stitches. This method will ensure an elastic edge that will stretch with the center section.

NUPPS

A nupp ("knob" or "button" in Estonian) is a bobble-like feature found in many Estonian lace patterns. Nupps are made up of 5, 7, or 9 stitches. Typically 7 stitches are used with fine- to medium-weight yarns, 5 stitches for thicker yarns, and 9 stitches for the finest yarns. There are various ways to make a nupp, but I consistently use the following method. To make a nupp on a right-side row, increase in a stitch by loosely knitting into the marked stitch, leave that stitch on the left needle, *yarnover and knit the stitch again (Figure 1); rep from * until you have 5, 7, or 9 stitches, ending with knitting the stitch to secure the last yarnover (Figure 2; 7 stitches shown). On the next row, purl the cluster of nupp stitches together (this is why it's important to work loosely) to return to the original number of stitches (Figure 3). An older variation is to make the increases on the wrong side of the work and knit them together through the back loop on the right side.

When working in rounds (as in when working a knitted-on edging), work the nupp increases on one round, then work the decrease on the following round by knitting the 5, 7, or 9 nupp stitches together through their back loops.

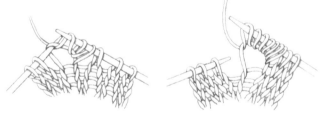

Figure 1   Figure 2

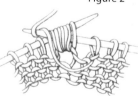

Figure 3

NUPP TIPS
Loose Tension

The best advice I can offer for making these small gems of Estonian lace knitting is keep the tension loose while making the nupp increases. I find it helpful to have a long length of yarn released from the ball so there isn't any extra tension on the yarn as you make the yarnovers. I also find it helpful to pinch the nupp stitches with the thumb and forefinger of the hand that isn't carrying the yarn to prevent the stitches from becoming tight as they are being made. It also helps if I pull up a bit on my right-hand needle to keep the increased stitches loose as I make them.

Too Many or Too Few Stitches

If you have too many stitches in a repeat section, check each nupp to be sure you worked all of the nupp stitches together on the following row. It's easy to miss a stitch when working the 5, 7, or 9 stitches together, and doing so will inadvertently add to the stitch count. If you notice a missed nupp loop, try to repair it right away. If you don't want to ravel back to the offending stitch, at least thread a length of working yarn through the missed stitch. Later, you can weave in the tails of the length of yarn on the wrong side of the shawl to secure the loop. Clip the ends of this yarn after the shawl has been blocked to prevent them from finding their way to the right side. If you find you are missing a stitch in a repeat, check to see if one stitch not intended to be part of the nupp was purled together when you completed the nupp on the wrong side. This is especially possible when there are yarnovers before or after the nupp stitches.

WEAVE IN LOOSE ENDS

If you don't plan on adding a lacy edge, weave in any loose ends into the wrong side of the garter-stitch frame, (where they will be less visible). Trim the ends, leaving 2" (5 cm) tails to be trimmed after the shawl is blocked. If you plan to sew on a lace edge, leave one tail at each corner (the lower left corner and the upper right corner as viewed from the right side) where the two halves of the lace edge will meet. These tails will be used to sew the corners of the lace edges together.

TRADITIONAL LACE EDGE

For a traditional Haapsalu shawl, the lace edge is knitted in two separate pieces that are sewn to the center section by hand. You can choose one of the patterns on pages 146–151 or an edging of your own. The most common edgings are 2" to 4" (5 to 10 cm) wide and most repeat over 10 stitches. Typically, ornate centers are combined with simple edges. The two parts of the lace edge are joined together at opposite corners of the center piece. If you prefer to work the lace edge in a single piece (which is not as common), there will be a single join at just one corner.

SPECIAL STITCHES

There are a few special knitting techniques, beyond the classic yarnovers and decreases that are found in Estonian lace patterns.

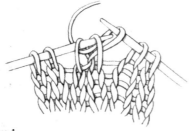

Figure 1

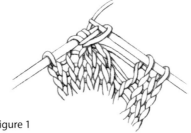

Figure 1

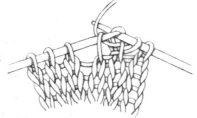

Figure 2

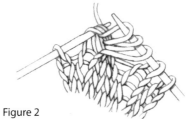

Figure 2

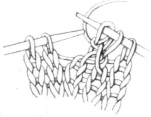

Figure 3

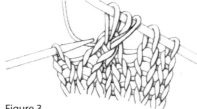

Figure 3

K2TOGTBL, K1, SLIP OFF BOTH STITCHES

Knit 2 stitches together through the back loop but leave the stitches on the left needle (Figure 1), knit into the first stitch as usual (2 stitches on right needle; Figure 2), then slip both stitches off the left needle (Figure 3).

(K3TOG, YO, K1) IN SAME STITCH

Knit 3 stitches together but leave these 3 stitches on the left needle (Figure 1), yarnover, then knit the same 3 stitches together again (3 stitches on right needle; Figure 2), then slip all 3 new stitches off the left needle (Figure 3).

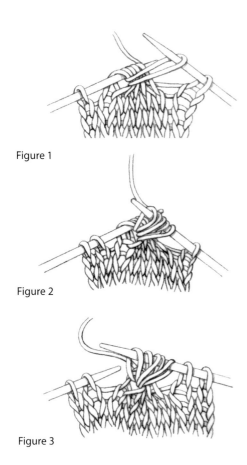

Figure 1

Figure 2

Figure 3

TAKE 5 STITCHES TOGETHER THEN MAKE 5 NEW STITCHES

Knit 5 stitches together but leave these 5 stitches on the left needle (Figure 1), yarnover, then knit the same 5 stitches together again, yarnover, then knit the same 5 stitches together again (5 stitches on right needle; Figure 2), then slip the original 5 stitches off the left needle (Figure 3).

Bind-Off

K2TOG BIND-OFF

The Estonians use a "k2tog" bind-off for all their lace knitting. The bind-off for the center of a shawl is worked with a single strand of yarn, as is the bind-off for the lace edge that will be sewn onto the shawl (the cast-on for this edge is worked with the yarn double). The bind-off for a lace edge that was picked up and knitted onto a center is worked with two strands held together. Slip the first stitch, knit the second stitch, *knit these 2 stitches together by inserting the left-hand needle into the front of them from left to right and knitting them together through their back loops with the right needle (Figure 1), then knit the next stitch (Figure 2); repeat from * until all of the stitches are secured. Cut the working yarn and pull up the last loop to secure the end of the bound-off stitches.

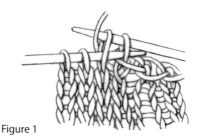

Figure 1

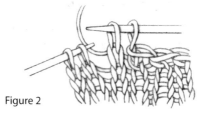

Figure 2

Join New Yarn

KNOTS

I have never advocated tying a knot in working yarns, however this procedure was advice I received in Haapsalu and, in this case, it seems to be a good idea, as a nupp could be used later to hide the knot. Tie a small knot, leaving long ends. Try to have the knot fall in a nupp and trim ends later. Tying a knot is not advisable when working a pattern that does not contain nupps.

OVERLAP ENDS

Thread one of the strands onto a yarn needle and use the needle to embed this strand into the other one (Figure 1), then trim the ends (Figure 2). This makes a secure overlap.

Figure 1

Figure 2

SPLICE

The splice method only works with pure wool or wool blended with other animal fibers. It does not work with silk, cotton, washable wool, and synthetic fibers. Ravel an inch or so of both the old and new ends of yarn (Figure 1). Moisten the ends (saliva works best, but use water if you prefer), overlap them (Figure 2), then quickly rub the overlapped section in your clean hands back and forth until the fibers stick together (Figure 3). This produces a semi-firm join that should be knitted carefully right away.

Figure 1

Figure 2

Figure 3

Calculate Stitch Count for Lace Edge

There are two ways to calculate the number of stitches to cast on for the lace edge. Each method gives roughly the same result, and I like to work through both to confirm that my calculations are correct.

To begin, you'll need to know the number of stitches across the width of the center piece, including the frame stitches. You'll also need to count the number of edge stitches along the length of the center piece, again including the frame rows. Because the first stitch of every row was slipped, there will be half as many edge stitches as there are rows of knitting. For example, if the center section is 300 rows long, there will be 150 edge stitches.

METHOD 1

This method calculates the total number of stitches needed for the entire length of the edge.

> **A** = number of stitches in width x 2
> **B** = number of edge stitches in length x 2
> **C** = A + B
> **D** = C ÷ 5
> **Ease at corners** = 18 extra stitches at each corner x 4 corners = 72
> **Total** = C + D + 72

You'll need to divide the total in half to get the number of stitches for each half of the edging (the top or bottom plus one side). Finally, round the resulting number up or down to achieve the closest stitch count that represents a full number of pattern repeats. For example, let's say that our shawl is 121 stitches wide and 150 edge stitches (300 rows) long, and let's say that we want to use a pattern with a 10-stitch-plus-1 repeat for the edging.

> **A** = 121 x 2 = 242
> **B** = 150 x 2 = 300
> **C** = 242 + 300 = 542
> **D** = 542 ÷ 5 = 108
> **Ease at corners** = 18 x 4 = 72
> **Total** = 542 + 108 + 72 = 722

To work the edging in two halves, divide 722 by 2 to get the number of stitches in each half (361). In this case, 361 stitches work perfectly for each half. To obtain a number that fits the 10-stitch lace pattern repeat evenly, we'd round down to 361 stitches for each half or up to 371 if out total were between 362 and 370.

METHOD 2

This method calculates the number of stitches needed for each half of the edge.

> **A** = number of stitches in width + 18 (for 2 corners)
> **B** = number of edge stitches on one side ÷ 3
> **C** = B x 4
> **D** = C + 18 (for 2 corners)
> **Total** = A + D

You'll need to round the total number up or down to be divisible by pattern repeat for the grand total. In our example, we have the following numbers:

A = 121 + 18 = 139
B = 150 ÷ 3 = 50
C = 50 x 4 = 200
D = 200 + 18 = 218
Total = 139 + 218 = 357

Rounding to the nearest number divisible by 10 + 1 gives us 361 stitches for each half—the same number calculated in the first method.

KNIT THE LACE EDGE

Cast on for the lace edge using the knitted cast-on (see page 23) as for the main piece, but work it with two strands of yarn held together to add weight and strength to this cast-on edge. The Haapsalu knitters may choose to use a needle one to two sizes larger than was used for the center for this cast on and a needle one size smaller than the cast-on needle for knitting the lace. However, I usually knit my shawls using the same size needle for the center and lace edgings. Break off one strand and continue with a single strand. Knit two rows. Begin the lace edge pattern at the point in the pattern where the lace edge scallops outward. For most edging patterns, this will occur along a line of double decreases. However, you'll want to begin the edge with a single decrease—"sl 1, k1,

psso" at the beginning of the row, and "k2tog" at the end of the row. The edge stitches on these lacy edges are not slipped. All subsequent decreases at this point in the repeat usually will be double decreases or two single decreases separated by a knit stitch. Most true Haapsalu lace edges are worked in garter stitch (right-side rows are pattern rows and wrong-side rows are simply knitted).

Work the lace edging for the desired width, then bind off with a single strand of yarn with the wrong side facing, using the k2tog method (see page 27).

JOIN LACE EDGE TO CENTER SECTION

The lace edge is always joined so that the widest part of a scallop is centered over two opposite corners and so that the two sections are joined at the other two opposite corners. (If the lace edge is made in one piece, there is a join at just one corner.) The two pieces are sewn onto the center with a single strand of yarn that is attached to the ball. The sewing is always done with the yarn attached to the ball instead of cutting a separate length (that may not be long enough to work the entire seam). The sewing yarn is not cut until both pieces of the lace edge have been attached and eased around all four corners to ensure that it will stretch as much as the knitted stitches.

RECTANGULAR SHAWLS

I learned the following method of sewing the lace to the center of a rectangular sall from Aime Edasi in Haapsalu.

Hold the edge of the center section between your thumb and index finger and the bind-off row of the lace edge between your index and middle fingers so that the right sides of the two pieces are facing together (Figure 1, page 32; the arrows show the direction the threaded needle will go through each piece). The center piece is closest to you. The arrows indicate the path of the needle while seaming. Begin at the lower left corner of the center piece (the left edge of the cast-on row). With the yarn from the ball threaded on a tapestry needle, bring the threaded needle from back to front through each of the first three loops of the lace edge (Figure 2), then through the first loop of the center piece from front to back (Figure 3). Repeat this three-one (3:1) ratio two more times (three times total)—nine stitches of the lace edge and three stitches of the center section have been joined (Figure 4). Next, take two loops from the lace edge and one loop from the center piece. Repeat this two-one ratio (2:1) two more times (three times total). Then work up the side of the shawl, alternating taking one loop from each piece two times, then two loops from the lace edge and one loop from the center piece (i.e., alternate 1:1, 1:1, 2:1) until you are 15 stitches from the center of the scallop on the lace edge that will form the corner and six stitches from the corner of the center section. Next, take two loops from the lace edge and one loop from the center piece three times, then take three loops from the lace edge and one loop from the center piece three times.

Because you rounded the number of stitches to cast-on for the edge to get full repeats of the lace pattern, you may need to make small adjustments in the sewing so that you end up at the corner stitch of the center piece and the exact center of a scallop on the lace edge. Make adjustments by taking more or fewer loops along the edge piece as needed; do not skip any loops on either piece or you'll end up with unsightly holes where the lace is attached to the center piece.

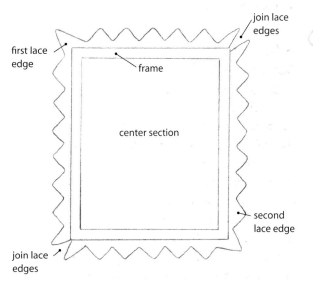

The lace edge is worked in two sections that are sewn to the edges of the frame. The widest part of the center scallop of each lace piece is centered over two opposite corners and the two sections are joined at the other two corners.

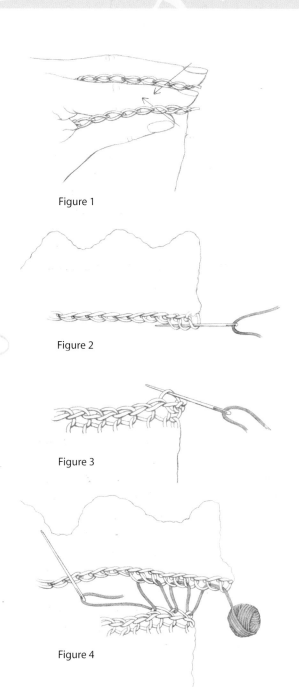

Figure 1

Figure 2

Figure 3

Figure 4

Continue this process for the top edge of the center piece: take three loops from the lace edge and one loop from the center piece three times, then take two loops from the lace edge and one loop from the center piece three times, then take one loop from each piece two times, alternating one loop from the lace edge and one loop from the center once (i.e., 1:1, 1:1, 1:2) until you are 15 stitches from the center of the scallop on the lace edge that will form the corner and six stitches from the corner of the center section. Take two loops from the lace edge and one loop from the center piece (2:1) three times, then take three loops from the lace edge and one loop from the center piece (3:1) three times to end up at the corner.

Join the other lace edge to the remaining two sides of the center in the same manner. When the entire lace edge is attached, sew the ends together using the yarn tails at the corners that were not woven in earlier. Do not sew the ends with the yarn used to attach the lace edge.

Carefully pull on the sewing yarn so there are no puckers, gathers, or tight spots in the seam between the center and lace edge, being careful not to pull the cut end of the sewing yarn through the sewn stitches. When you are satisfied that the lace edge is eased evenly all around, cut the sewing yarn from the ball. Wait to weave in the ends until after the shawl has been blocked.

SQUARE SHAWLS

The following method for sewing the lace edge to the center of a square shawl comes from *Haapsalu Räti-kud* by Linda Elgas. Linda recommends to work the corners as for rectangular shawls, but for the areas between the corners, take one stitch from the lace edge and one stitch from the center three times then two stitches from the lace edge and one from the center once (i.e,.1:1, 1:1, 1:1, 2:1). This system is worked between the corners on all sides.

For a square shawl, it is necessary to work an even number of repeats for the lace edge. This will allow for the same number of "points" on the edge between the corners, one point at each corner (made up of a whole repeat at two of the corners and half repeats, sewed together to make a whole repeat, at the other two corners; or whole points at three corners and two half repeats at the last corner if you knitted the edge in a single piece). You may need to adjust your calculated stitch count to achieve this. If the number you calculated for the number of stitches to cast on is close to the number that will give you an even number of repeats, round to the nearest number. If it is right in the middle, round up to the number that will give an even number of repeats. For example, if your total is 111 stitches, round up to 121 (12 repeats of 10 stitches plus 1 stitch).

FINISHING

Wash the shawl in warm water (the Estonians use rain water) and a mild soap. Squeeze gently, rinse and squeeze again, never wring. While the shawl is still wet, "dress" (block) it on a frame made of wooden boards with nails at even intervals that are lashed together at the corners or pin it out onto a carpet covered with a sheet or towel (see page 35). An alternative that isn't used in Estonia but is popular among American knitters is to use blocking wires. Either way, allow the shawl to thoroughly air-dry before moving it, then weave in the loose ends.

CONTEMPORARY KNITTED-ON LACE EDGE

Although the traditional Haapsalu sall has a sewn-on lace edge and the knitters in Haapsalu believe that is the "correct" way to make a shawl, other Estonian knitters pick up stitches around the edges of the center section and work the lace edge in the round. This method is described in Leili Reimann's books, and I suspect it was developed with the invention of circular knitting needles, as this type of edge couldn't be worked on single-point needles. I think of this way of adding a lace edge as a contemporary or modern edge treatment. The corners are formed by miters in which increases are worked into the pattern at each corner to allow the edge to lay flat. I learned this method of adding edges to shawls from my friend Hilja Aavik, a very skilled lace knitter and teacher from Tallinn.

Begin by choosing a center stitch pattern, knitting a sample to determine your gauge, and deciding on the number of stitches to cast-on, including frame stitches as described for the traditional method on pages 29–30.

In preparation to pick up stitches for the edging, the center section begins with a provisional cast-on (see page 37). Using a smooth cotton yarn in a contrasting color, make a crochet chain at least 10 loops longer than the number of stitches you want to cast on. Cut the yarn and pull the tail through the last loop to secure it. Tie a knot in this tail so you'll be able to find it later. With the working yarn and beginning and ending several loops from the ends of the chain, pick up and knit one stitch in each bump on the underside of the chain until you have the required number of stitches.

Edge Stitches

Except for the very first row after the cast-on, begin every row with a slipped stitch (knit the first stitch of the first row) to form a selvedge edge that's easy to see when picking up stitches later. Slip this stitch purlwise with the yarn in front, then return the yarn to the back between the two needles in preparation to knit the next stitch (see page 23).

Center Pattern

Beginning with a few rows of garter stitch, work the center pattern as for a traditional shawl (see page 22), ending having worked the last row of the pattern repeat (a wrong-side row), then work a few rows of garter stitch. Do not bind off the stitches.

Lace Edge

For the lace edge to be worked in the round, a circular needle is needed. A few rounds of garter stitch are sometimes worked after the edge is picked up, followed by the lace pattern in which a patterned round is followed by a plain knit round to produce a stockinette-stitch background. To produce a garter-stitch background for the lace edge, purl the rounds between the patterned rounds. Although purling alternate rounds produces a garter-stitch ground that gives the same look as the traditional shawls (in which the edging is worked separately and sewn in place), this is rarely done by Estonian knitters.

Determine the number of stitches needed in your pattern repeat for the edge (for example, a multiple of 10 stitches plus 2 stitches for each of the four sides of the shawl). With a circular needle and the right side of the center facing, knit across the stitches at the top of the piece (the stitches that are still on the needle), placing a unique marker after the first stitch and increasing 10 to 15 more stitches (whatever is needed to give the correct stitch count for the pattern) to give some fullness at the top. Next, pick up and knit

BLOCKING FRAME

The frame for blocking a square or rectangular shawl consists of four wooden boards, each measuring 1" (2.5 cm) by 2" (5 cm) by 50" to 80" (130 to 200 cm), depending on the knitted dimensions. The wood must be dry, lightweight, and sap free. Birch is most commonly used. Stainless steel or brass nails (about 3" [7.5 cm] long) are nailed to the center of the 2" (5 cm) surface, at about 2" to 2½" (5 to 6 cm) intervals, and so that about 2" (5 cm) of the nail extends above the wood. Strips of cloth or thin rope are used to tie the four boards together at the corners.

The wet shawl is mounted onto the nails at each point in the lace edge. Before you begin, check to make sure that the boards are long enough to accommodate the size of your shawl. If not, you'll need a larger frame or pin the shawl to the floor. Tie the boards together at the corners to make a stable frame. Loop the points of the shawl over the nails, working around the shawl point by point. If the spacings between the points of the lace edge don't match the spacings of the nails, thread metal needles or strong blocking wires through each point, then hook the needles or wires over the nails. Estonian knitters tend to use the same edge pattern over and over and set up their boards specifically for their patterns.

An alternate method is to place the wet shawl on top of a clean bed sheet on a padded surface on the floor (a padded carpet works well) and pin out each of the points to the padded surface. For straight edges that don't have lace points, thread blocking wires through each selvedge stitch to keep them straight while drying. Place pins at regular intervals along the inner edge of the wires to hold the wires at the desired width and length.

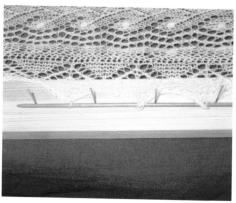

PHOTOS BY NANCY BUSH

stitches along the left side of the center, placing another marker after the first stitch. Pick up with a ratio of three stitches for every two selvedge stitches (see page 38) along the entire selvedge edge to end with about a third more stitches picked up than there are selvedge stitches. For a fuller edge, pick up one stitch from the first stitch, two from the second stitch, and two from the third stitch, and repeat along the entire selvedge edge.

When you reach the cast-on edge, you'll need to remove the waste yarn to expose the live stitches from the provisional cast-on at the bottom of the center piece. Find the knotted tail of the crochet chain, carefully pull this end of the waste yarn out of the last crocheted stitch, then gently pull the waste yarn to expose the cast-on stitches one at a time and

place these stitches onto an empty needle. Count the stitches to make sure that you've picked up one live stitch for every stitch that was picked up in the chain. Knit across these stitches, increasing the same number of stitches as you did at the top edge and placing a third marker after the first stitch.

Pick up stitches along the other selvedge edge as before, placing a fourth marker after the first picked-up stitch on this edge and ending at the upper right corner of the center section.

The stitch before each marker is a corner stitch, which is where increases will be worked to miter the corners. The unique-colored marker after the first corner stitch is to alert you that you are at the beginning of the round as well as to mark the first corner stitch.

FINISH THE LACE EDGE

If the shawl has a lace edge, pick up each doubled outer edge stitch on the lace edge with a knitting needle, all around the shawl and pull on it slightly to open up the edge stitches. This rounds the points of the lace edge and is very important. Carefully fold the dry shawl so that the points of the lace edge line up with opposite points. Estonian knitters traditionally place a pillow on top of the folded shawl and allow it to "rest" for several hours or overnight.

Rather than using live stitches for the corners, you may pick up one new stitch at each of these corner points, including the picked-up stitches in the stitch count. Always use markers at each corner to keep track of these important corner stitches.

You may purl one round, then knit one round, then purl one more round. These few rows of garter stitch obscure the picked-up and increased stitches around the perimeter of the center section. Or, you may simply begin the lace edge pattern on the next round. I have seen shawls from Estonia done either way.

Follow the pattern for the lace edge, remembering to alternate each pattern round with a plain knit (or purl) round, and increasing at each corner as indicated until there are a full number of pattern repeats. Work four or six rounds (or more) in pattern as established without increasing at the corners. Complete when edge is desired width and end having worked an even-numbered round.

Bind Off
Use the k2tog bind-off (see page 27) with the yarn doubled. This doubled outer edge gives strength and adds weight to the finished shawl, just as the doubled cast-on does for the traditional style shawl. Cut the yarn and pull the tail through the loop to secure.

Wash and block as for a traditional shawl (see page 35).

Cast On
CROCHET CHAIN PROVISIONAL CAST-ON
This is the method I was taught in Estonia by Hilja Aavik, my first Estonian lace teacher. Using a contrast color yarn, preferably cotton, begin by making a crochet chain at least 10 loops longer than your required stitch count. Pull the tail up through the last loop to secure it. Tie a knot in the tail so that you'll be able to find it later. With working yarn, pick up and knit the required stitches in the bumps in the underside of the chain (Figure 1), beginning and ending several loops from each end of the chain. When it's time to expose the loops of the picked-up stitches, find the knotted tail of the contrast yarn, unloop it from the last crochet stitch, then pull this tail to expose the live stitches (Figure 2), placing them on a needle as you go.

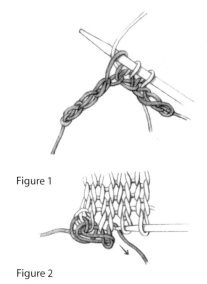

Figure 1

Figure 2

PICKING UP SELVEDGE STITCHES

Pick up and knit stitches along the selvedges by picking up three stitches for every two selvedge stitches. To do this pick up one stitch under both loops of the first chain stitch (Figure 1), one stitch under just the back loop of the second chain stitch (Figure 2), then one stitch under both loops of the same chain stitch (Figure 3). Continue in this manner along the entire selvedge edge. You will end with about a third more stitches than there are selvedge stitches. For a fuller edge, pick up one stitch from the first stitch, two from the second stitch, and two from the third stitch, and repeat this sequence along the entire selvedge edge.

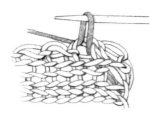

Figure 1

Figure 2

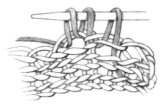

Figure 3

THREE-NEEDLE BIND-OFF

This join can be used in place of the Kitchener stitch for ending triangular shawls that are worked from the bottom edge up. But be aware that this creates a more obvious seam. Place the stitches to be joined onto two separate needles and hold the needles parallel so that the right sides of the knitting face together. Insert a third needle into the first stitch on each of the two needles (Figure 1) and knit them together as one stitch (Figure 2), *knit the next stitch on each needle the same way, then use the left needle tip to lift the first stitch over the second and off the needle (Figure 3). Repeat from * until no stitches remain on the first two needles. Cut the yarn and pull the tail through the last stitch to secure.

Figure 1

Figure 2

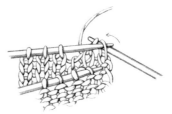

Figure 3

KITCHENER STITCH

As far as I know, the Estonians don't use this technique for joining shawl pieces. On the shawls that I own, the top or bottom edges are sewed to the center, which is subtly visible and has less elasticity than the knitting. I chose to use the Kitchener stitch in these cases to form an invisible seam with the same stretch as the knitted rows. Arrange the stitches on two needles so that there is the same number of stitches on each needle. Hold the needles parallel to each other with wrong sides of the knitting together. With yarn threaded on a tapestry needle, work from right to left as follows:

Step 1. Bring the tapestry needle through the first stitch on the front needle as if to purl and leave the stitch on the needle (Figure 1).

Step 2. Bring the tapestry needle through the first stitch on the back needle as if to knit and leave that stitch on the needle (Figure 2).

Step 3. Bring the tapestry needle through the first front stitch as if to knit and slip this stitch off the needle, then bring tapestry needle through the next front stitch as if to purl and leave this stitch on the needle (Figure 3).

Step 4. Bring the tapestry needle through the first back stitch as if to purl and slip this stitch off the needle, then bring tapestry needle through the next back stitch as if to knit and leave this stitch on the needle (Figure 4).

Repeat Steps 3 and 4 until 1 stitch remains on each needle, adjusting the tension to match the rest of the knitting as you go. To finish, bring the tapestry needle through the front stitch as if to knit and slip this stitch off the needle, then bring the tapestry needle through the back stitch as if to purl and slip this stitch off the needle.

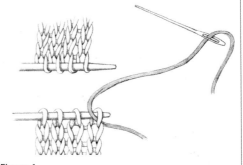

Figure 1

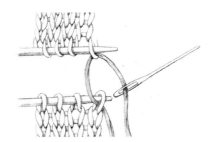

Figure 2

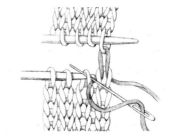

Figure 3

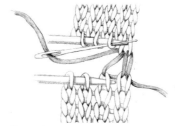

Figure 4

Queen Silvia Shawl

This classic pattern was named for Queen Silvia of Sweden. It is a variation on the Lily of the Valley motif and includes an openwork flower motif between the sprigs of buds and gathered stitches above each set of sprigs. The lace edge on this shawl is picked up and knitted on, in the modern technique. The edge pattern is a variation of the classic "yo, k1, yo, k3, sl 1, k2tog, psso, k3" pattern that uses a k2 between each double decrease and its companion yarnovers instead of a k3. I chose to purl the even-numbered rounds to mimic the look of the garter-stitch-ground edges on traditional shawls.

Finished Size

About 24" (61 cm) wide and 58" (147.5 cm) long, relaxed after blocking.

Yarn

Laceweight (#0 Lace).

Shown here: Skacel Merino Lace (100% wool; 1375 yd [1250 m]/100 g): #426 natural white, 1 skein.

Needles

Size U.S. 3 (3.25 mm): straight and 36" (90 cm) circular (cir). Adjust needle size if necessary to obtain the correct gauge.

Notions

Smooth cotton waste yarn; size G/6 (4.25 mm) crochet hook; 4 markers (m; three the same color and one in a different color); tapestry needle.

Gauge

10 stitches and 19 rows = 2" (5 cm) in stockinette stitch, before blocking; 20-stitch pattern repeat from Silvia Center chart measures about 3¾" (9.5 cm) wide, relaxed after blocking.

STITCH GUIDE

5-Stitch Nupp

Working very loosely, work (k1, yo, k1, yo, k1) all in same st—
5 nupp sts made from 1 st. On the foll row, purl the 5 nupp sts
tog (as shown on chart)—5 nupp sts dec'd back to 1 st.

Gathered Stitches (worked over 5 sts)

K5tog but do not slip sts from needle, yo, knit the same
5 sts tog again but leave on needle, yo, knit the same
5 sts tog once more, then slip all 5 sts from needle.

Note

~ Slip the first stitch of each row as if to purl
  with yarn in front (pwise wyf), except for the
  first stitch of the first row in the center section,
  which is worked as k1.

Silvia Center

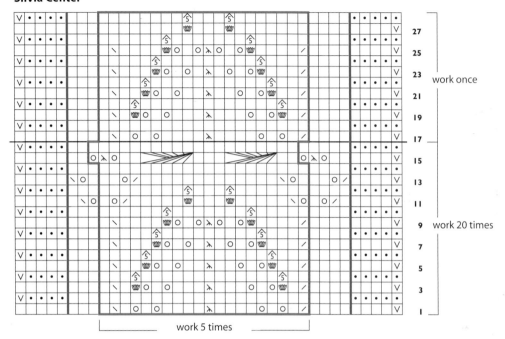

work once

work 20 times

work 5 times

- ○ yo
- ╱ k2tog
- ╲ sl 1, k1, psso
- ⋋ sl 1, k2tog, psso
- ♛ 5-st nupp (see Stitch Guide)
- ⌃ p5tog
- V sl 1 (see Note)
- ▨ edging corner st
- ▦ no stitch
- ☐ pattern repeat
- | marker position
- ⟫⟫⟫ gathered sts (see Stitch Guide)

Silvia Lace Edge

corner st

CENTER RECTANGLE

With cotton waste yarn and crochet hook, chain about 130 sts (see page 37). Tie a knot in the end of the cotton after the last chain so you'll be able to identify this end later. With straight needles and working yarn, pick up and knit 117 sts from the center 117 "bumps" along the back of the crochet chain. Work 8 rows in garter st, knitting the first st of the first row, but slipping the first st of every row thereafter (see Note). Rep Rows 1–16 of Silvia Center chart 20 times, placing markers (pm) after the first 5 sts and before the last 5 sts, slipping the first st of every row as before, and keeping rem sts outside markers in garter st. Work Rows 17–28 of chart once—332 chart rows total. Slipping the first st of every row as established, knit 8 rows, ending with a WS row. Leave sts on needle and do not cut yarn.

LACE EDGE

With cir needle and RS facing, k1 (corner st), pm of different color to indicate beg of rnd, knit to end and *at the same time* inc 13 sts evenly spaced—130 sts. With RS still facing, pick up and knit 1 st (corner st) from left selvedge, pm, then pick up and knit (see page 38) 257 sts along rem selvedge—258 sts total picked up along left selvedge. Beg at knotted end, carefully remove the waste-yarn crochet chain, placing each live st on empty straight needle as it becomes free—117 sts from CO edge. With RS facing and cir needle, work across sts from CO edge as foll: K1 (corner st), pm, knit to end and *at the same time* inc 13 sts evenly spaced—130 sts from CO edge. With RS still facing, pick up and knit 1 st (corner st) from right selvedge, pm, then pick up and knit 257 sts along rem selvedge—776 sts total: 130 sts each at upper and lower edges, 258 sts along each side. The stitch before each marker is a corner st. When working Silvia Lace Edge chart, start each side at the beg of the chart with the corner st (shown in gold). Establish patt from Rnd 1 of Silvia Lace Edge chart as foll: *K1 (corner st of short side), slip marker (sl m), yo, work marked 8-st patt rep 16 times, k1, yo, k1 (corner st of long side), sl m, yo, work marked 8-st patt rep 32 times, k1, yo; rep from * once more for rem 2 sides of shawl—1 st inc'd each side of each of the 4 corner sts. Work Rnds 2–14 of chart—832 sts after completing Rnd 7: 144 sts along top and lower edges, 272 sts along each side. Join a second strand of yarn and loosely BO all sts with 2 strands held tog using the k2tog method (see page 27).

FINISHING

Handwash gently in mild soap and warm water. Pin shawl out to about 26" (66 cm) wide and 60" (152.5 cm) long, pinning out each [yo, k1, yo] point of the lace edge. When dry, weave in loose ends.

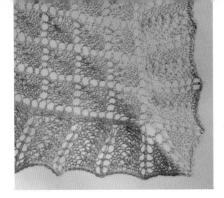

TRIANGULAR SCARF
in LEAF PATTERN

This scarf is adapted from one I purchased in Estonia that I reach for when I need just a little extra warmth around my shoulders, whether I want a dressy or casual look. The main triangle is worked in a traditional allover leaf pattern and begins with a few stitches at the point, then increases steadily at the sides until it reaches the final width across the top edge. Stitches for the lace edging are picked up around all three sides of the triangle are worked in rounds outward to the scalloped points. The pattern for the edging is a "modern" classic one, with plain knit rounds worked every other round to create a stockinette-stitch ground.

Finished Size
About 52"(132 cm) wide across top edge and 32" (81.5 cm) long from center of top edge to tip of lower point.

Yarn
Laceweight (#0 Lace).
Shown here: Habu Textiles 100% A-169 Naturally Dyed Cashmere 2/24 (100% cashmere; 187 yd [171 m]/ ½ oz [14.2 g]): #14 dusty plum, 3 skeins (with very little left over).

Needles
Size U.S. 2 (2.75 mm): straight. Edging—size U.S. 3 (3.25 mm): 32" (80 cm) circular (cir). Adjust needle size if necessary to obtain the correct gauge.

Notions
Markers (m; two the same color, one in a different color); tapestry needle.

Gauge
12 stitches and 18 rows = 2" (5 cm) in stockinette stitch on smaller needles, before blocking; 24 stitches and 48 rows (three pattern repeats wide and three repeats high) of Leaf center chart measure about 4½" (11.5 cm) wide and 6" (15 cm) high, after blocking.

Notes

~ For triangle section of scarf, slip the first stitch of every row purlwise with yarn in front (pwise wyf).

~ Each time you repeat Rows 17–32 of the Leaf Center chart enough stitches will have been increased to work the marked 8-stitch pattern repeat two more times than before. For example, when you work Rows 17–32 the first time, there will only be enough stitches to work the marked repeat section once. Because the stitch count increases by 2 stitches every RS row, or 16 stitches every 16 rows, each time you work Rows 17–32, there will be enough stitches to work the 8-stitch pattern repeat an additional two times. When you work Rows 17–32 the second time, there will be enough stitches to work the 8-stitch pattern repeat three times, then on the following Rows 17–32, there will be enough stitches to work the pattern repeat five times, and so on. The 13th and final time you work Rows 17–32 there will be enough stitches to work the 8-stitch pattern repeat 25 times. The repeat shown in Rows 33–40 is also worked 25 times.

☐	k on RS; p on WS
·	p on RS; k on WS
○	yo
↧	k1f&b
\	sl 1, k1, psso
⅄	sl 1 kwise, k2tog, psso
∨	sl 1 (see Notes)
▓	edging corner st, knit every rnd
▒	no stitch
☐	pattern repeat

CENTER TRIANGLE

With smaller needles and using the knitted method (see page 23), CO 3 sts. Work Rows 1–32 of Leaf Center chart once (see page 53 for row-by-row instructions to get started)—37 sts. Rep Rows 17–32 of chart 12 more times (see Notes)—229 sts. Work Rows 33–40 of chart once—237 sts; 232 chart rows completed. Work 6 more rows as foll:

Row 1: (RS) Sl 1, k2, yo, k1, *yo, k2tog; rep from * to last 3 sts, yo, k3—239 sts.

Row 2: Sl 1, k2, purl to last 3 sts, k3.

Rows 3 and 5: Sl 1, k2, yo, knit to last 3 sts, yo, k3—243 sts after Row 5.

Rows 4 and 6: Sl 1, knit to end—238 rows total from beg; piece measures about 26½" (67.5 cm) from CO, unblocked and measured straight up at center.

Leave sts on needle and do not cut yarn.

LACE EDGE

With cir needle and RS facing, k243 across top of shawl and *at the same time* inc 9 sts evenly spaced—252 sts. Pm

Leaf Lace Edge

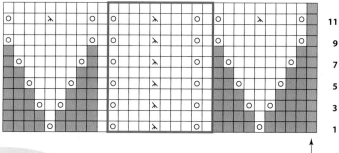

corner st

(one of the two of the same color), pick up and knit 242 sts along selvedge to lower point of triangle (about 2 sts for every slipped selvedge st; see page 38), pm (the other of the same color), pick up and knit 242 sts along rem selvedge, pm (different color) to denote beg of rnd—736 sts total. The first st after every marker is a corner st. When working Leaf Lace Edge chart, start each side of the triangle at the beg of the chart with the corner st (shown in gold). Establish pattern from Rnd 1 of Leaf Lace Edge chart as foll: K1 (corner st), yo, work marked 10-st patt rep 25 times, k1, yo; *slip marker (sl m), k1 (corner st), yo, work marked 10-st patt rep 24 times, k1, yo; rep from * once more—1 st inc'd on each side of each of the 3 corner sts. Work Rnds 2–12 of chart—790 sts: 270 sts in first section for top edge, and 260 sts in each of next 2 sections for sides. Join a second strand of yarn and BO all sts with 2 strands held tog using the k2tog method (see page 27).

FINISHING

Handwash gently with mild soap and warm water. Pin scarf out to desired measurements, pinning out each [yo, k1, yo] point in the edging. When dry, weave in loose ends.

Leaf Center

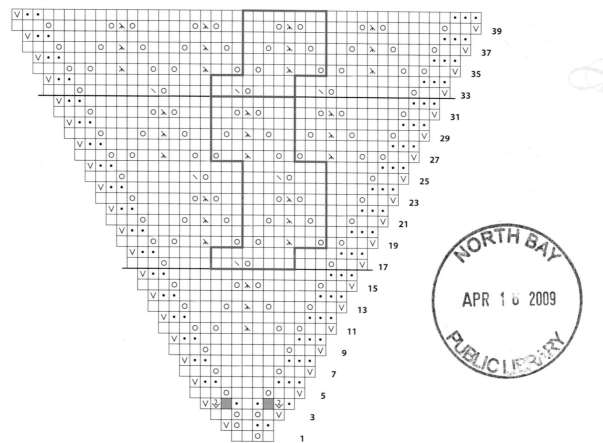

ROW-BY-ROW INSTRUCTIONS FOR LEAF CENTER CHART ROWS 1–18

Row 1: K1, yo, k2—4 sts.

Row 2: Sl 1, yo, p1, k2—5 sts.

Row 3: Sl 1, [k1, yo] 2 times, k2—7 sts.

Row 4: Sl 1, knit into the front and back of next st (k1f&b), k1, p1, k1, k1f&b, k1—9 sts.

Row 5: Sl 1, k2, [yo, k3] 2 times—11 sts.

Rows 6, 8, 10, 12, 14, and 16: Sl 1, k2, purl to last 3 sts, k3.

Row 7: Sl 1, k2, yo, k5, yo, k3—13 sts.

Row 9: Sl 1, k2, yo, k7, yo, k3—15 sts.

Row 11: Sl 1, k2, yo, k1, yo, k2, sl 1 kwise, k2tog, psso, k2, yo, k1, yo, k3—17 sts.

Row 13: Sl 1, k2, yo, k3, yo, k1, sl 1 kwise, k2tog, psso, k1, [yo, k3] 2 times—19 sts.

Row 15: Sl 1, k2, yo, k5, yo, sl 1 kwise, k2tog, psso, yo, k5, yo, k3—21 sts.

Row 17: Sl 1, k2, yo, k7, yo, sl 1, k1, psso, k6, yo, k3—23 sts.

Row 18: Sl 1, k2, p17, k3.

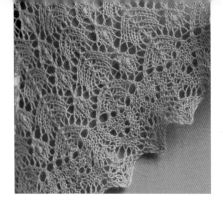

PEACOCK TAIL
and LEAF SCARF

This design was inspired by a shawl in the collection of the Estonian National Museum. The shawl, knitted in wool by Frieda Terts (1911–1997), came to the Museum in 1991 from the Estonian House in Toronto, Canada. Frieda emigrated to Canada where she was very active in the Ethnographic Society in Toronto. This design is a beautiful example of the lace tradition carried on outside Estonia. The scalloped lace edging on the short ends of the scarf is separated from the main section by garter-stitch bands punctuated with holes. The long sides have narrow garter-stitch bands that are pinned out at even intervals during blocking to produce scalloped edges.

Finished Size
About 15" (38 cm) wide and 49" (124.5 cm) long, after blocking.

Yarn
Fingering weight (#1 Super Fine).
Shown here: Wooly West Horizons Lace Yarn (100% wool; 525 yd [480 m]/50 g): willow (greenish tan), 1 skein.

Needles
Size U.S. 3 (3.25 mm). Adjust needle size if necessary to obtain the correct gauge.

Notions
Markers (m); stitch holder; removable marker or safety pin; tapestry needle.

Gauge
11 stitches and 20 rows = 2" (5 cm) in stockinette stitch, before blocking; 24 stitches and 40 rows (two pattern repeats wide and four pattern repeats high) of Peacock Center chart measure about 4¾" (12 cm) wide and 5½" (14 cm) high, after blocking.

Notes

~ The scarf is worked in one piece from the lower edging to the end of the center section. The top edging is worked separately so its direction of knitting will match the lower edging, then the two pieces are grafted together with the Kitchener stitch.

~ When working the top edging, you may find it helpful to mark the right side of the work with a removable marker or safety pin so you can be sure to match the right sides of the two pieces when grafting.

~ A double strand of yarn is used for the cast-on, then a single strand is used for the remainder of the scarf.

STITCH GUIDE

7-Stitch Nupp

Working very loosely, work ([k1, yo] 3 times, k1) all in same st—7 nupp sts made from 1 st. On the foll row, purl the 7 nupp sts tog as shown on chart—7 nupp sts dec'd back to 1 st.

SCARF

Lower Edging

With double strand of yarn and using the knitted method (see page 23), CO 81 sts. Cut off one strand of yarn and cont with a single strand only. Knit 2 rows. Work Rows 1–12 of Peacock Edging chart. Knit 4 rows, dec 10 sts evenly spaced on last row—71 sts rem. **Eyelet row:** (RS) K1, *yo, k2tog; rep from * to end. Knit 1 WS row.

Center Section

Work Rows 1–10 of Peacock Center chart 32 times, placing markers (pm) after the first 5 sts and before the last 5 sts, slipping the first st of every row as if to purl with yarn in front (pwise wyf), and keeping rem sts outside markers in garter st. Knit 2 rows. **Eyelet row:**

Peacock Center

work 4 times

Legend

☐	k on RS; p on WS
•	p on RS; k on WS
o	yo
∕	k2tog
＼	sl 1, k1, psso
⋏	sl 1, k2tog, psso
⏝	7-st nupp (see Stitch Guide)
⋏	p7tog
V	sl 1 pwise wyf (see instructions)
☐	pattern repeat
❘	marker position

Peacock Edging

work 7 times

55

PEACOCK TAIL AND LEAF SCARF

(RS) K1, *yo, k2tog; rep from * to end. Knit 3 rows, inc 10 sts evenly spaced on last row, and ending with a WS row—81 sts. Cut yarn, leaving a 12" (30.5 cm) tail. Place sts on holder, or set aside if you have an extra set of needles to use for the top edging.

Top Edging

With double strand of yarn and using the knitted method (see page 23), CO 81 sts. Cut off one strand of yarn and cont with a single strand only. Knit 2 rows. Work Rows 1–12 of Peacock Edging chart, using a removable marker or safety pin to mark the RS if desired (see Notes), and ending with a WS row. Cut yarn, leaving a 12" (30.5 cm) tail.

Join Center Section to Top Edging

If necessary, return held center section sts to needle with RS facing and needle tip pointing to the right.

Hold center section and top edging tog with RS facing outward, WS facing tog, and both needle tips pointing to the right. Thread the yarn attached to the ball on a tapestry needle, and use the Kitchener st (see page 39) to graft the two pieces together, adjusting the tension of the stitches to match the tension of the knitting. Cut grafting yarn and weave in its ends, leaving 2" (5 cm) tails that will be trimmed after blocking.

FINISHING

Handwash gently with mild soap and warm water. Pin shawl to finished measurements, pinning out each [sl 1, k2tog, psso] point along the top and bottom edgings, and pinning out the sides about every 3" (7.5 cm) to create a scalloped effect as shown. When dry, weave in loose ends and trim ends of grafting yarn flush with surface of scarf.

LEHE SQUARE SHAWL

For this square shawl, I wanted to use a very traditional border pattern. I settled on a pattern from *Haapsalu Ratik*, published by the Federated Estonian Woman's Clubs in New York in 1972. The border was called *Lehemustriline Poort I*, or Leaf Pattern Border 1. I continued the nature theme into the center section by choosing an allover leaf pattern, which I found in the book *Silmus Kudumine* by Claire Hallik. The lace edge is a contemporary one that I worked by picking up stitches around all four sides of the shawl and knitting outward. The pattern I chose for the lace edge is a popular one found on many shawls and scarves made in Estonia today.

Finished Size
About 42" (106.5 cm) square, relaxed after blocking.

Yarn
Fingering weight (#1 Super Fine).
Shown here: Jamieson and Smith Shetland 2-Ply Laceweight (100% wool; 185 yd [169 m]/25 g): #L1A natural white, 6 skeins.

Needles
Size U.S. 5 (3.75 mm): straight and 32" (80 cm) or longer circular (cir). Adjust needle size if necessary to obtain the correct gauge.

Notions
Smooth cotton waste yarn for provisional cast-on; markers (m; four the same color, one in a different color); size G/6 (4.25 mm) crochet hook; tapestry needle.

Gauge
11½ stitches and 16 rows = 2" (5 cm) in stockinette stitch, before blocking; 16-stitch pattern repeat from Lehe Top and Bottom Border chart measures about 4¼" (11 cm) wide, relaxed after blocking; 20 stitches and 32 rows (two pattern repeats wide and two pattern repeats high) of leaf pattern from Lehe Center chart measure about 4¾" (12 cm) wide and 4½" (11.5 cm) high, relaxed after blocking.

Notes

~ The center section of this shawl is worked in one piece from lower border to top border.

~ Stitches for the lace edging are picked up and knit around all four sides of the completed center square and worked outward.

~ Slip the first stitch of each row as if to purl with yarn in front (pwise wyf), except for the first stitch of the first row in the center section, which is worked as k1.

CENTER SQUARE

With cotton waste yarn and crochet hook, chain about 150 sts (see page 37). Tie a knot in the end of the cotton after the last chain to identify this end later. With straight needles and working yarn, pick up and knit 141 sts from the center 141 "bumps" along the back of the crochet chain. Work 10 rows in garter st, knitting the first st of the first row, but slipping the first st of every row thereafter (see Notes), ending with a WS row. **Next row:** (RS) Sl 1, knit to end, placing same-color markers (pm) after the first 5 sts and before the last 5 sts.

Next row: (WS) Sl 1, k4, purl to last 5 sts, k5. Establish patt from Lehe Top and Bottom Border chart on next RS row as foll: Work 5 sts before marker (m) as established, work Row 1 of chart over center 131 sts, work 5 sts after m in garter st as established. Cont to work edgings outside m as established, work Rows 2–28 of chart. Establish patts from side border and center charts on next RS row as foll: Work first 5 sts as established, work Row 1 of Lehe Side Border chart over next 19 sts, pm, work Row 1 of Lehe Center chart over next 93 sts, pm, work Row 1 of Lehe Side Border chart over next 19 sts, work last 5 sts as established. On the foll rows, for side border chart work Rows 2–28 once, then work Rows 1–28 five more times; for center chart, work Rows 2–12 once, then work Rows 13–28 nine times, then work Rows 29–40 once—168 patt rows total from beg of Lehe Side Border and Lehe Center charts. Change to Lehe Top and Bottom Border chart, and working 5 sts at each side as established, work Rows 1–28 of chart over center 131 sts. **Next row:** (RS) Sl 1, knit to end. **Next row:** (WS) Sl 1, k4, purl to last 5 sts, k5. Slipping first st of each row as established, work 10 rows garter st, ending with a WS row.

LACE EDGE

With cir needle and RS facing, k1 (corner st), pm of different color to indicate beg of rnd, knit to end, inc 41 sts evenly spaced as you go—182 sts. With RS still facing, pick up and knit (see page 38) 1 st (corner st) from left selvedge, pm, then pick up and knit 181 sts along rem selvedge (about 3 sts for every 2 slipped edge sts)—182 sts total picked up along left selvedge. Beg at knotted end, carefully remove the waste-yarn crochet chain, placing each live st on empty straight needle as it becomes free—141 sts from CO edge. With RS facing and cir needle, work across sts from CO edge as foll: K1 (corner st), pm, knit to end, inc 41 sts evenly spaced as you go—182 sts from CO edge. With RS still facing, pick up and knit 1 st (corner st) from right selvedge, pm, them pick up and knit 181 sts along rem selvedge—728 sts total: 182 sts along each side; the st before each marker is a corner st. When working lace edge, start each side at the beg of the chart with the corner st (shown in gold). Establish patt from Rnd 1 of Lehe Lace Edge chart as foll: *K1 (corner st), slip marker (sl m), yo, work marked 10-st patt rep 18 times, k1, yo; rep from * 3 more for rem 3 sides of shawl—1 st inc'd on each side of each of the 4 corner sts. Work Rnds 2–16 of chart—800 sts after completing Rnd 9: 200 sts along each side. Join a second strand of yarn and loosely BO all sts with 2 strands held tog using the k2tog method (see page 27).

FINISHING

Handwash gently with mild soap and warm water. Pin shawl out to about 44" (112 cm) square, pinning out each [yo, k1, yo] point along the lace edge; finished piece will relax to about 42" (106.5 cm) square. When dry, weave in loose ends.

Lehe Lace Edge

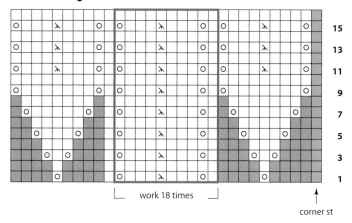

work 18 times

corner st

Lehe Side Border

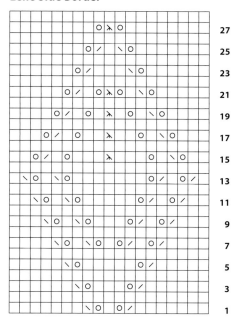

Lehe Top and Bottom Border

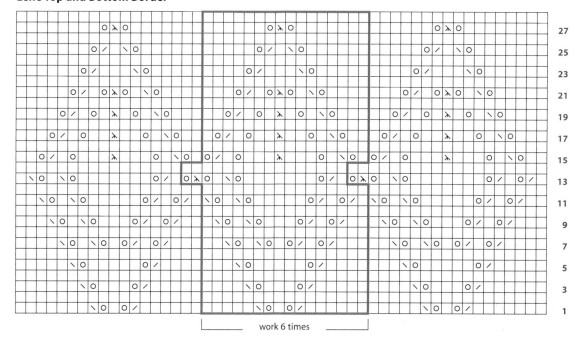

work 6 times

Lehe Center

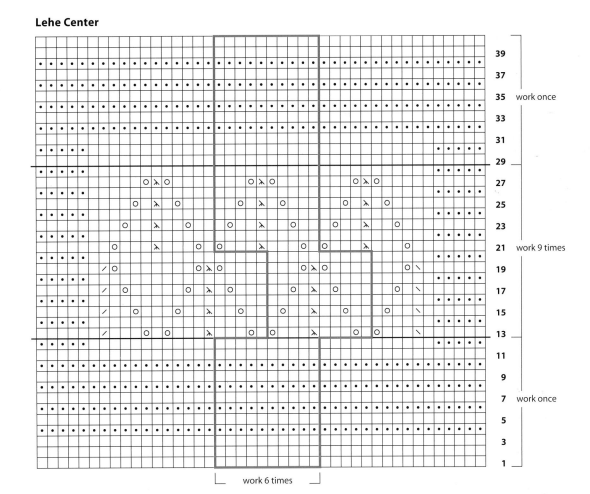

work once

work 9 times

work once

work 6 times

	k on RS; p on WS
•	p on RS; k on WS
O	yo
∕	k2tog
∖	sl 1, k1, psso
入	sl 1, k2tog, psso
	edging corner stitch
	no stitch
	pattern repeat

RAHA SCARF

I got the idea for this scarf from my editor and friend, Ann Budd. She thought it might be interesting to knit a scarf using only one repeat of a pattern for the width. When I came across this pattern, I knew it would be perfect for such a scarf. The *Rahakiri* or Money pattern is one of the oldest Haapsalu patterns mentioned in the literature I have found. This pattern came to me from the knitting ladies in Haapsalu, and they have told me they "think" it is the Raha pattern. In any case, it's an interesting departure from the leaf and lily patterns.

Finished Size
About 5½" (14 cm) wide and 53" (134.5 cm) long, relaxed after blocking.

Yarn
Fingering weight (#1 Super Fine).
Shown here: Moco Yarns 45% Qiviut/45% Merino/10% Silk Fingering Weight (45% musk ox qiviut, 45% merino, 10% silk; 220 yd [201 m]/1 oz [28.5 g]): DL-SUF100 suntan, 1 skein.

Needles
Size U.S. 4 (3.5 mm). Adjust needle size if necessary to obtain the correct gauge.

Notions
Markers (m); tapestry needle.

Gauge
13 stitches and 16 rows = 2" (5 cm) in stockinette stitch, before blocking; 21 pattern stitches from center of Raha chart (not including garter edge sts) measure 4¼" (11 cm) wide, relaxed after blocking.

SCARF

Using the knitted method (see page 23), CO 29 sts. Slipping the first st of every row pwise with yarn in front (wyf), work in garter stitch for 5 rows, beg and ending with a RS row. **Next row:** (WS) Sl 1, k3, place marker (pm), k21, pm, k4. Slipping the first st of every row as before, work Rows 1–6 of Raha chart once, then work Rows 7–38 eleven times, then work Rows 39–65 once—385 chart rows total. Slipping first st of every row as before, work in garter st for 6 rows, ending with a RS row. With WS facing and using the k2tog method (see page 27), loosely BO all sts.

FINISHING

Handwash gently with mild soap and warm water. Pin scarf out (or use blocking wires) to about 7" (18 cm) wide and 56" (142 cm) long to block; finished piece will relax to about 5½" (14 cm) wide and 53" (134.5 cm) long. When dry, weave in loose ends.

Raha

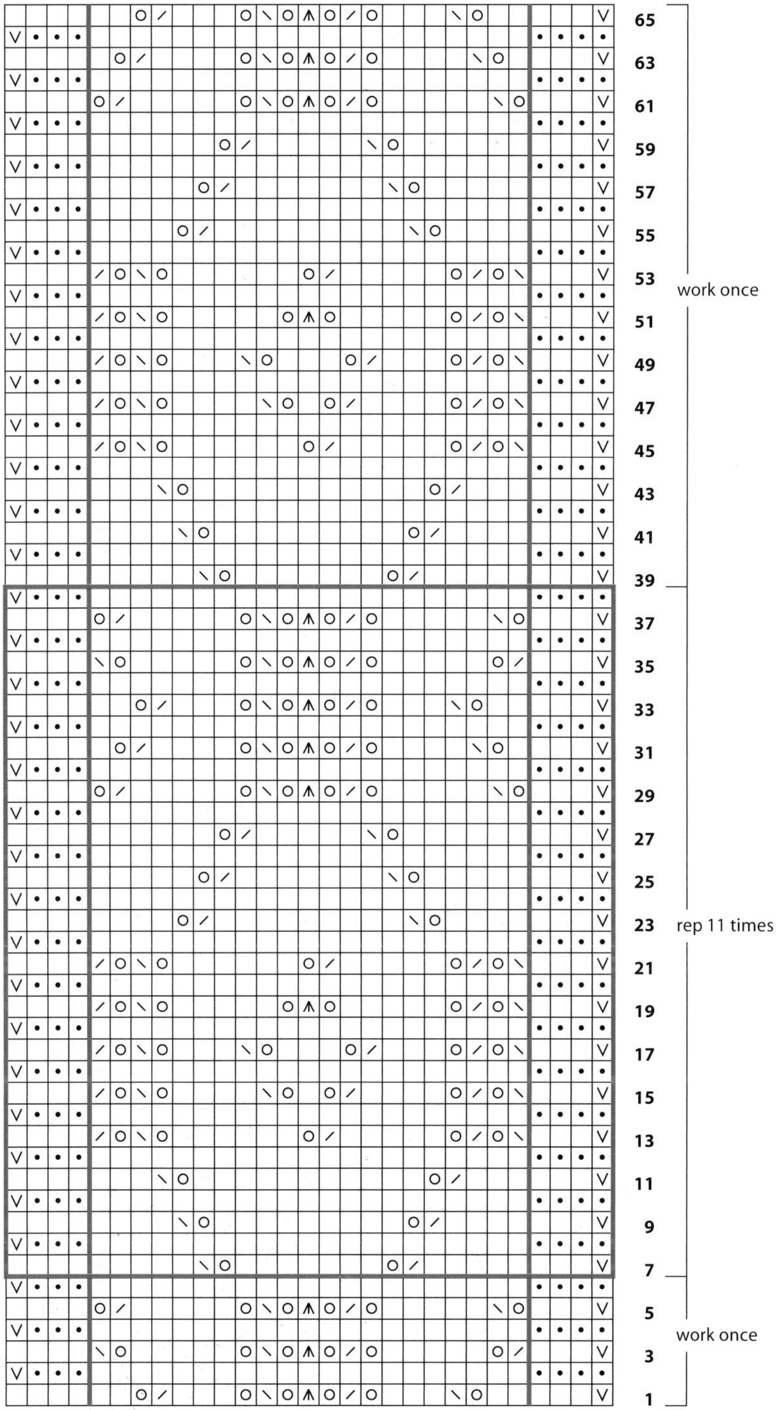

65

Row labels (bottom to top): 1, 3, 5, 7, 9, 11, 13, 15, 17, 19, 21, 23, 25, 27, 29, 31, 33, 35, 37, 39, 41, 43, 45, 47, 49, 51, 53, 55, 57, 59, 61, 63, 65

work once

rep 11 times

work once

Legend

□	k on RS; p on WS
•	p on RS; k on WS
╱	k2tog
╲	sl 1, k1, psso
○	yo
∨	sl 1 (see instructions)
⋀	sl 2 as if to k2tog, k1, p2sso
▢	pattern repeat
▮	marker position

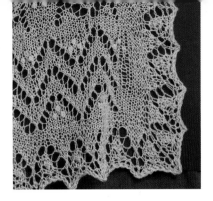

LEAF *and* NUPP SHAWL

This delightful shawl was inspired by one in the collection of the Estonian National Museum in Tartu. The pattern is a mix of garter stripes embellished with nupps and a double leaf motif and bordered with a very decorative openwork zigzag at the top and bottom. I began the shawl with a crochet-chain provisional cast-on and worked the main part of the shawl up to the top. The lace edge is picked up around all four sides and knitted on in the more modern style. I used a pattern similar to ones used where the lace edge is sewn onto the shawl, reworked it to fit nicely around the corners, and knitted it with a garter-stitch ground (purling every even-numbered round) to mimic the look of many traditional shawls.

Finished Size
About 22" (56 cm) wide and 60" (152.5 cm) long, after blocking.

Yarn
Fingering weight (#1 Super Fine).
Shown here: Wooly West Horizons Lace Yarn (100% wool; 525 yd [480 m]/50 g): sandhill (taupe), 1 skein.

Needles
Size U.S. 3 (3.25 mm): straight and 32" (60 cm) or longer circular (cir) for edge. Adjust needle size if necessary to obtain the correct gauge.

Notions
Smooth cotton waste yarn for provisional cast-on; markers (m; three the same color, one in a different color); size G/6 (4.25 mm) crochet hook; tapestry needle.

Gauge
9 stitches and 14 rows = 2" (5 cm) in stockinette stitch, before blocking; 22 stitches and 20 rows (one pattern repeat wide and one pattern repeat high) of Leaf and Nupp Center chart measure about 4¾" (12 cm) wide and 3¼" (8.5 cm) high, after blocking.

STITCH GUIDE

7-Stitch Nupp

Working very loosely, work ([k1, yo] 3 times, k1) all in same st—7 nupp sts made from 1 st. On the foll row, purl the 7 nupp sts tog as shown on chart—7 nupp sts dec'd back to 1 st.

Notes

~ The center section of this shawl is worked in one piece from lower border to top border. Stitches for the lace edging are picked up and knit around all four sides of the completed center rectangle and worked outward.

~ Slip the first stitch of each row as if to purl with yarn in front (pwise wyf), except for the first stitch of the first row in the center section, which is worked as k1.

SHAWL

Center Section

With cotton waste yarn and crochet hook, chain about 85 sts (see page 37). Tie a knot in the end of the cotton after the last chain to identify this end easily later. With straight needles and working yarn, pick up and knit 75 sts from the center 75 "bumps" along the back of the crochet chain. Work 6 rows in garter st, knitting the first st of the first row, but slipping the first st of every row thereafter (see Notes), ending with a WS row. Work Rows 1–25 of Leaf and Nupp Border chart, placing same-color markers (pm) after the first 4 sts and before the last 4 sts, and ending with a RS row. **Next row:** (WS) Sl 1, k3, purl to last 4 sts, k4. **Next 3 rows:** Knit,

slipping the first st of each row, and beg and ending with a RS row. **Next row:** (WS) Sl 1, knit to end, repositioning markers after the first 8 sts and before the last 8 sts. Change to Leaf and Nupp Center chart and work Rows 1–8 once, then work Rows 9–28 fourteen times, then work Rows 29–39 once, ending with a RS row—299 chart rows completed. **Next 4 rows:** Knit, slipping the first st of each row, repositioning markers after the first 4 sts and before the last 4 sts in the first row, and ending with a RS row. **Next row:** (WS) Sl 1, k3, purl to last 4 sts, k4. Work Rows 1–25 of Leaf and Nupp Border chart, ending with a RS row. **Next 5 rows:** Knit, slipping the first st of each row, and ending with a WS row—370 rows total from CO. Do not break yarn.

Lace Edge

With cir needle and RS facing, k1 (corner st), pm of different color to indicate beg of rnd, knit to end, inc 7 sts evenly spaced as you go—82 sts. With RS still facing, pick up and knit 1 st (corner st) from left selvedge, pm, then pick up and knit (see page 38) 273 sts along rem selvedge (about 3 sts for every 2 slipped edge sts)—274 sts total picked up along left selvedge. Beg at knotted end, carefully remove the waste-yarn crochet chain, placing each live st on empty straight needle as it becomes free—75 sts from CO edge. With RS facing and cir needle, work across sts from CO edge as foll: K1 (corner st), pm, knit to end, inc 7 sts evenly spaced as you go—82 sts from CO edge. With RS still facing, pick up and knit 1 st (corner st) from right selvedge, pm, pick up and knit 273 sts along rem selvedge—712 sts total: 82 sts each at upper and lower edges, 274 sts along each side; the st before each marker is a corner st. Purl 1 rnd, slipping markers as you come to them. **Note:** When working the edge, start each side at the beg of the chart with the corner st (shown in gold).

Establish patt from Rnd 1 of Leaf and Nupp Lace Edge chart as foll: *K1 (corner st of short side), slip marker (sl m), yo, k1, work marked 8-st patt rep 9 times, yo, sl 1, k1, psso, k3, k2tog, yo, k1, yo, k1 (corner st of long side), sl m, yo, k1, work marked 8-st patt rep 33 times, yo, sl 1, k1, psso, k3, k2tog, yo, k1, yo; rep from * once more for rem 2 sides of shawl—8 sts inc'd; 1 st inc'd on each side of all 4 corner sts. Work Rnds 2–9 of chart—736 sts after completing Rnd 5; 88 sts along top and lower edges, 280 sts along each side. Purl 1 rnd, then knit 1 rnd. Join a second strand of yarn and loosely BO all sts with 2 strands held tog using the k2tog method (see page 27).

FINISHING

Handwash gently with mild soap and warm water. Pin shawl out to finished measurements, pinning out each [yo, k1, yo] point of the edging. When dry, weave in loose ends.

KNITTED LACE OF ESTONIA

□	k on RS; p on WS
·	p on RS; k on WS
o	yo
/	k2tog
\	sl 1, k1, psso
⋏	k3tog
人	sl 1, k2tog, psso
⑭	7-st nupp (see Stitch Guide)
↑	p7tog
v	sl 1 pwise wyf (see Notes)
▨	edging corner stitch
▥	no stitch
□	pattern repeat
∣	marker position

Leaf and Nupp Lace Edge

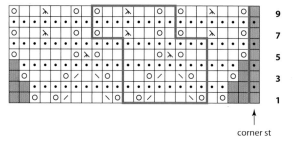

corner st

Leaf and Nupp Border

work 4 times

Leaf and Nupp Center

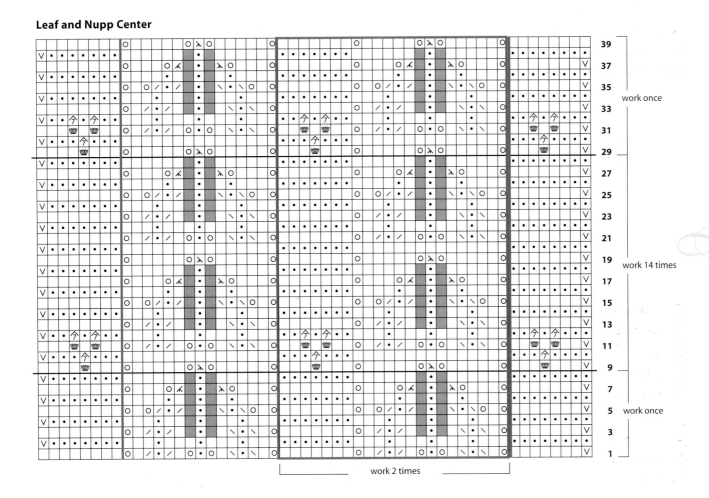

Maikell Shawl

This shawl is made with the traditional Haapsalu construction method. The stitches for the center are cast on and worked to the desired length, then the stitches are bound off on the wrong side. The lace edge is then knitted in two parts, each of which is sewn separately onto the center. I used a shawl I purchased in Haapsalu as my inspiration for this shawl and have had many lessons during my visits there to learn the details of this type of construction.

Finished Size
About 25" (63.5 cm) wide and 46" (117 cm) long, after blocking.

Yarn
Laceweight (#0 Lace).
Shown here: Omaghi Filati Merino Oro (100% wool; 1375 yd [1250 m]/100 g): #028 natural, 1 skein.

Needles
Shawl Center—size U.S. 3 (3.25 mm): straight. Lace Edge—size U.S. 4 (3.5 mm): straight. Lace Edge Cast-On—size U.S. 5 (3.75 mm): straight. Adjust needle size if necessary to obtain the correct gauge.

Notions
Markers (m); safety pin or removable marker; tapestry needle.

Gauge
10 stitches and 19 rows = 2" (5 cm) in stockinette stitch with smallest needles, before blocking; 28-stitch pattern repeat from Maikell Center chart measures about 5¼" (13.5 cm) wide with smallest needles, after blocking.

STITCH GUIDE

7-Stitch Nupp

Working very loosely, work ([k1, yo] 3 times, k1) all in same st—7 nupp sts made from 1 st. On the foll row, purl the 7 nupp sts tog (as shown on chart)—7 nupp sts dec'd back to 1 st.

Twisted Sts (worked over 2 sts)

K2tog through the back loop (tbl) but do not slip sts from left needle, insert needle tip between the 2 sts just worked tog and knit the first st again, then slip both sts from left needle.

Notes

~ The center of the shawl is worked in one piece. The lace edge is worked in two identical pieces that are sewn to the center section.

~ A double strand of yarn is used for the lace edge cast-on, then a single strand is used for the remainder of lace edge.

~ Right-side Rows 13–24 of the Center chart intentionally do not contain the same number of twisted-stitch sets at each side: there are two sets at the beginning of these rows and only one set at the end of these rows.

SHAWL CENTER

With middle-size needles and single strand of yarn, use the knitted method (see page 23) to CO 121 sts. Change to smallest-size needles. Knit all sts for 6 rows—3 garter ridges. Work Rows 1–24 of Maikell Center chart a total of 12 times, placing markers (pm) after the first 4 sts and before the last 4 sts, slipping the first st of every row as if to purl with yarn in front (pwise wyf), and keeping rem sts outside markers in garter st—288 chart

rows completed. Knit all sts for 7 rows, beg and ending with a RS row. With WS facing and single strand of yarn, and using the k2tog method (see page 27), BO all sts. Set aside.

LACE EDGE (MAKE 2)

With yarn doubled and largest-size needles, CO 361 sts. Cut off one strand of yarn and cont with a single strand only. Change to middle-size needles. Use a safety pin or removable marker to mark the RS of the piece. Knit all sts for 2 rows. Work Rows 1–8 of Maikell Lace Edge chart (do not slip the edge sts). Knit 1 RS row across all sts. Using the k2tog method, BO all sts. Make a second lace edge the same as the first.

Join Lace Edge to Center

Hold the center section and one lace edge with RS tog and so that the center piece is closest to you. With the yarn from the ball threaded on a tapestry needle and beg at the lower left corner of the center piece (the left edge of the CO row), sew the two pieces tog (see page 30) as foll: Bring the threaded needle from back to front through each of the first 3 loops of the lace edge, then through the first loop of the center piece from front to back. Rep this 3:1 ratio 2 more times (3 times total)—9 sts of lace edge and 3 sts of center have been joined. Next, take 2 loops from the lace edge and 1 loop from the center piece. Rep this 2:1 ratio 2 more times (3 times total). Work along the side of the shawl by taking [1 loop from the lace edge and 1 loop from the center (1:1) 2 times, then 2 loops from the lace edge and 1 loop from the center one time (2:1)]—i.e., 1:1, 1:1, 2:1—until 15 sts rem before the center of the scallop that will form the corner and 6 sts rem before the next corner of the center section. Next, take 2 loops from the lace edge and 1 loop from the center (2:1) 3 times, then take 3 loops from the lace edge and 1 loop from the center (3:1) 3 times. **Note:** You may need

to make small adjustments (by taking more or fewer sts along the lace edge; do not skip sts on either piece or holes will form) in the sewing to end up exactly at the center of a scallop of the lace edge and the corner of the center section. Cont this process across the top of the shawl: work the 3:1 ratio 3 times, then the 2:1 ratio 3 times, then the 1:1, 1:1, 2:1 ratio until 15 sts rem from the center of the scallop that will form the corner and 6 sts rem before the corner of the center section. Then, work the 2:1 ratio 3 times, then the 3:1 ratio 3 times to end up at the corner. Join the other lace edge to the rem 2 sides of the center section in the same manner, beg along the side and ending across the bottom of the shawl. Using a tail from the center section or separate length of yarn, sew the lace edgings tog at the corners. Check to make sure there are no puckers or tight areas in the seam before cutting the seaming yarn.

FINISHING

Handwash gently in mild soap and warm water. Pin shawl out to desired measurements, pinning out each [sl 1, k2tog, psso] point along the lace edge. When dry, weave in loose ends.

Maikell Center

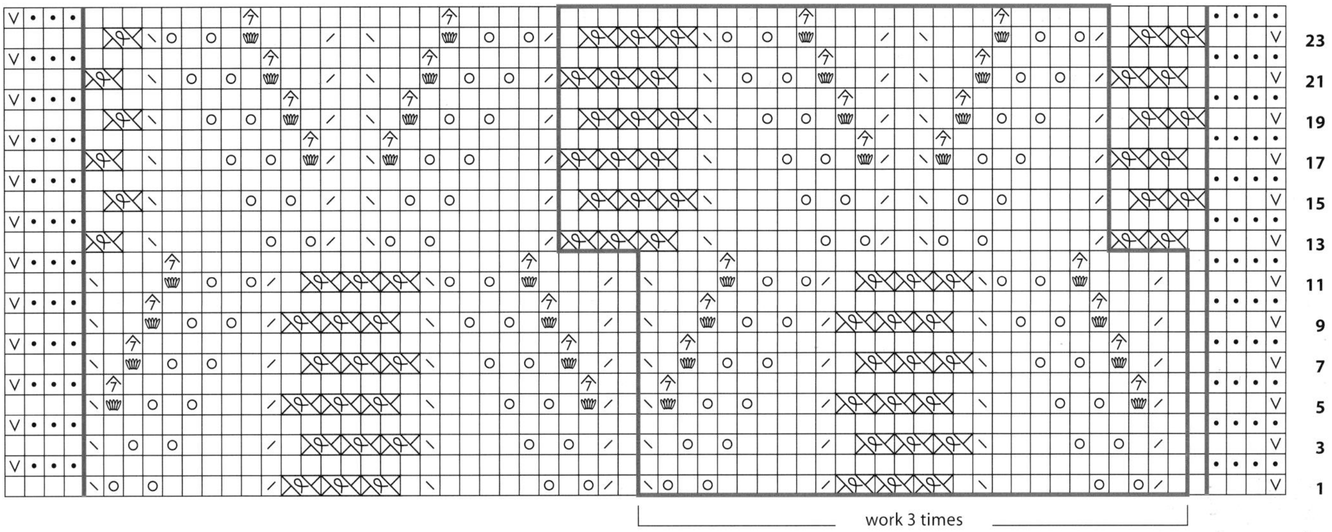

23
21
19
17
15
13
11
9
7
5
3
1

work 3 times

Legend:

☐	k on RS; p on WS
•	p on RS; k on WS
○	yo
╱	k2tog
╲	sl 1, k1, psso
⋏	sl 1, k2tog, psso
♛	7-st nupp (see Stitch Guide)
↑	p7tog
V	sl 1 pwise wyf
⋈	twisted sts (see Stitch Guide)
☐	pattern repeat
❘	marker position

Maikell Lace Edge

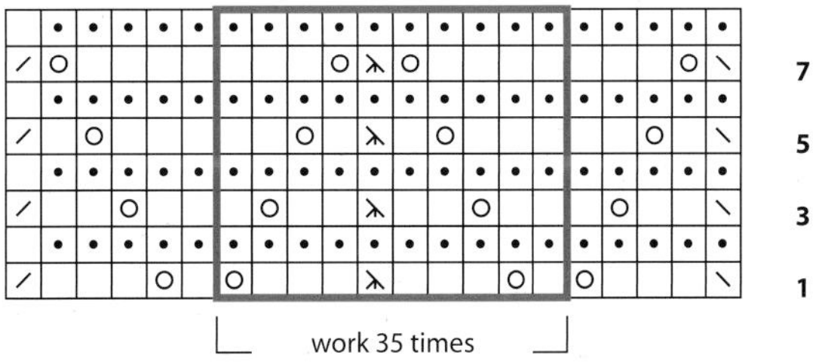

7
5
3
1

work 35 times

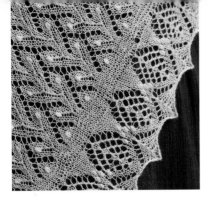

MADLI'S SHAWL

This shawl, reworked in finer yarn than the original pattern in the Summer 2004 issue of *Interweave Knits*, was named for Madli Puhvel, author of *Symbol of Dawn*, the biography of the beloved nineteenth-century Estonian poet Lydia Koidula. Madli has also provided me valuable support and friendship as I researched this book. The pattern in the main section of this shawl is a version of the *Haga*, (twig or small branch) pattern to which I have added nupps for texture.

Finished Size
About 14" (35.5 cm) wide and 56" (142 cm) long, relaxed after blocking.

Yarn
Laceweight (#0 Lace).
Shown here: Yarn Place Gentle (95% wool, 5% cashmere; 1,380 yd [1,262 m]/100 g): #13 dusty pink, 1 skein.

Needles
Size U.S. 4 (3.5 mm): straight. Adjust needle size if necessary to obtain the correct gauge.

Notions
Markers (m); stitch holder; tapestry needle.

Gauge
15 stitches and 21 rows = 2" (5 cm) in stockinette stitch, before blocking; 36 stitches and 48 rows (three pattern repeats wide and four pattern repeats high) of Madli Center chart measure about 5¼" (14 cm) wide and 6" (15 cm) high, after blocking.

STITCH GUIDE

7-Stitch Nupp

Working very loosely, work ([k1, yo] 3 times, k1) all in same st—7 nupp sts made from 1 st. On the foll row, purl the 7 nupp sts tog as shown on chart—7 nupp sts dec'd back to 1 st.

Notes

~ The shawl is worked in one piece from the lower border to the end of the center section. The top lace edge is worked separately so its direction of knitting will match the lower lace edge, then the two pieces are grafted together with the Kitchener stitch.

~ A double strand of yarn is used for the cast-on, then a single strand is used for the remainder of the shawl.

LOWER LACE EDGE

With double strand of yarn and using the knitted method (see page 23), CO 101 sts. Cut off one strand of yarn and cont with a single strand only. Knit 2 rows. Work Rows 1–26 of Madli Lace Edge chart, slipping the first st of every row as if to purl with yarn in front (pwise wyf). Knit 7 rows, ending with a RS row. **Next row:** (WS) Knit, inc 1 st after the first 4 sts and inc 1 st before the last 4 sts—103 sts.

CENTER SECTION

Work Rows 1–12 of Madli Center chart 31 times, placing markers (pm) after the first 5 sts and before the last 5 sts, slipping the first st of every row pwise wyf, and keeping rem sts outside markers in garter st. Knit

6 rows. **Next row:** (WS) Knit, dec 1 st after the first 4 sts and dec 1 st before the last 4 sts, removing side markers as you come to them—101 sts rem. Cut yarn, leaving a 12" (30.5 cm) tail. Place sts on holder or set aside if you have an extra set of needles to use for the top edging.

TOP LACE EDGE

With double strand of yarn and using the knitted method, CO 101 sts. Cut off one strand of yarn and cont with a single strand only. Knit 2 rows. Work Rows 1–25 of Madli Lace Edge chart, slipping the first st of every row pwise wyf; do not work Row 26. Knit 1 WS row. Cut yarn, leaving a 2 yd (1.8 m) tail.

Join Center Section to Top Lace Edge

If necessary, return held center section sts to needle with RS facing and needle tip pointing to the right. Hold center section and top lace edge tog with RS facing outward, WS facing tog, and both needle tips pointing to the right. Thread long tail from top lace edge on a tapestry needle, and use the Kitchener st (see page 39) to graft the two pieces together, adjusting the tension of the stitches to match the tension of the knitting. Cut grafting yarn and weave in its end, leaving a 2" (5 cm) tail that will be trimmed after blocking.

FINISHING

Handwash gently with mild soap and warm water. Pin shawl out to about 17" (43 cm) wide and 64" (162.5 cm) long to block, pinning out each [sl 1, k1, psso, k1, k2tog] point and side edges of the borders; finished piece will relax to about 14" (35.5 cm) wide and 56" (142 cm) long. When dry, weave in loose ends and trim end of grafting yarn flush with surface of shawl.

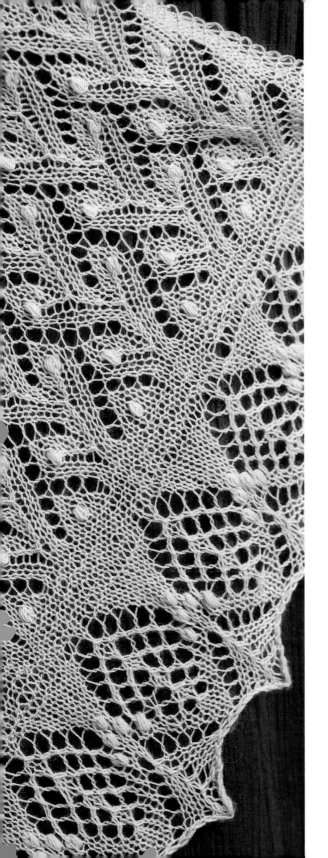

Madli Center

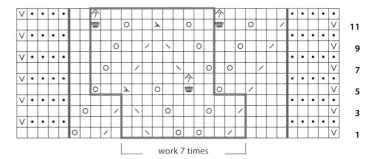

work 7 times

Madli Lace Edge

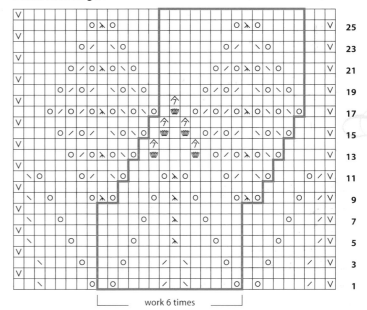

work 6 times

	k on RS; p on WS		7-st nupp (see Stitch Guide)
•	p on RS; k on WS		p7tog
O	yo	V	sl 1 pwise wyf (see instructions)
/	k2tog		pattern repeat
\	sl 1, k1, psso		marker position
⋏	sl 1, k2tog, psso		

TRIANGULAR SUMMER SHAWL

This shawl, designed by Helve Poska, has been published in issue #121 of *Triinu* magazine, in the *Suvi* (Summer) of 1983 and by the Estniska Etnografiska Föreningen (Estonian Ethnographical Society) in Sweden in 1986. Helve gave me permission to use it here. Instead of being shaped by decreasing evenly from the top (cast-on) edge to the tip, the decreases are worked at each end of every right-side row for about half the length, then at each end of every row thereafter to create slightly angled sides. I modified the original pattern by adding a few rows of garter stitch after the lace edge at the top and a garter-stitch edging along each side. I also added more stitches to the lace edge that is sewn onto the two lower sides to give a more rounded shape to the three corners.

Finished Size
About 56" (142 cm) wide across top edge and 24" (61 cm) long from center of top edge to tip of lower point, relaxed after blocking.

Yarn
Laceweight (#0 Lace).
Shown here: Wooly West Horizons Lace Yarn (100% wool; 525 yd [480 m]/50 g): natural white, 2 skeins.

Needles
Size U.S. 4 (3.5 mm): 32" (60 cm) circular (cir). Adjust needle size if necessary to obtain the correct gauge.

Notions
Markers (m); removable marker or safety pin; tapestry needle.

Gauge
11½ stitches and 22 rows = 2" (5 cm) in stockinette stitch, before blocking; 30 stitches (two 15-st pattern repeats) from Summer Center charts measures about 6¼" (16 cm) wide, relaxed after blocking.

STITCH GUIDE

7-Stitch Nupp

Working very loosely, work ([k1, yo] 3 times, k1) all in same st—7 nupp sts made from 1 st. On the foll row, purl the 7 nupp sts tog (as shown on chart)—7 nupp sts dec'd back to 1 st.

Notes

~ The shawl begins with the lace edge at the top (long) edge. The center section has a 4-stitch garter-stitch border along each of the angled lower sides. The lace edge for the lower sides is knitted separately and sewn to the center section during finishing.

~ When shaping the main section, one stitch is decreased inside the 4-stitch garter edgings every right-side row until Row 59, then beginning with Row 60, one stitch is decreased at each side every row to Row 138.

CENTER

Top Lace Edge

With yarn doubled and using the knitted method (see page 23), CO 251 sts. Cut off one strand of yarn and cont with a single strand only. Knit 2 rows. Work Rows 1–11 of Summer Lace Edge chart. Slipping the first st of each row as if to purl with yarn in front (pwise wyf), knit 2 rows, ending with a RS row. **Next row:** (WS) Sl 1, knit to end and *at the same time* dec 14 sts evenly spaced—237 sts rem. Slipping the first st of each row as established, knit 2 rows, ending with a WS row.

Center Section

Work Rows 1–64 of Summer Center Chart 1, placing markers (pm) after the first 4 sts and before the last 4 sts, slipping the first st of every row, and keeping rem sts outside markers in garter st (see Notes)—167 sts rem. Maintaining 4 sts at each end of needle as established, work Rows 65–96 of Summer Center Chart 2—103 sts rem. Maintaining 4 sts at each end of needle as established, work Rows 97–128 of Summer Center Chart 3—39 sts rem. Cont as foll:

Row 129: (RS) Sl 1, k3, sl 1, k1, psso, knit to last 6 sts, k2tog, k4—2 sts dec'd

Row 130: Sl 1, k3, p2tog, purl to last 6 sts, sl 1, p1, psso, k4—2 sts dec'd.

Rows 131–135: Rep Rows 129 and 130 two times, then work Row 129 once more—25 sts rem.

Row 136: (WS) Sl 1, k3, k2tog, knit to last 6 sts, sl 1, k1, psso, k4—2 sts dec'd.

Row 137: Sl 1, k3, sl 1, k1, psso, knit to last 6 sts, k2tog, k4—2 sts dec'd.

Row 138: Rep Row 136—19 sts rem.

Row 139: Sl 1, knit to end.

With a single strand of yarn, loosely BO all sts using the k2tog technique (see page 27).

LACE EDGE (MAKE 1)

With yarn doubled and using the knitted method, CO 271 sts. Cut off one strand of yarn and continue with a single strand only. Knit 2 rows (do not slip the first st of the rows of the lace edge). Place a removable marker or safety pin on the right side of the piece. Work Rows 1–11 of Summer Lace Edge chart. Knit 2 rows, ending with a RS row. With a single strand of yarn, BO all sts using the k2tog technique.

Join Lace Edge to Center

With right sides of both pieces facing up, distribute the lace edge around the center section, matching the midpoint of the lace to the center of the 19 BO sts of the center and matching the "half points" at the ends of the lace tog with the ends of the top lace edge to form a continuous piece. Hold the center section and lace edge with RS tog and so that the center section is closest to you. Using a single strand of yarn attached to the ball threaded on a tapestry needle, sew the lace edge to the center as foll (see page 30): Working from top to lower edge, take 1 st from the lace edge and 1 st from the center (1:1) once, then take 2 sts from the lace edge and 1 st from the center (2:1) once. Rep this sequence to the 19 BO sts at the "point." Work across these sts taking 3 sts from the lace edge and 1 from the center (3:1) 19 times. Cont up the other side, alternating 1:1 and 2:1 to the top corner.

Using a tail or separate length of yarn, sew the ends of the lace edging tog. Check to make sure there are no puckers or tight areas in the seam before cutting the seaming yarn.

FINISHING

Handwash gently with mild soap and warm water. Pin shawl out to about 64" (162.5 cm) across the top edge and 24" (61 cm) from center of top edge to tip of lower point, pinning out each [sl 1, k2tog, psso] point along the lace edges; finished piece will relax to about 56" (142 cm) wide across the top. When dry, weave in loose ends.

Legend:

□	k on RS; p on WS
·	p on RS; k on WS
o	yo
/	k2tog on RS; p2tog on WS
\	sl 1, k1, psso on RS; sl 1, p1, psso on WS
⋋	sl 1, k2tog, psso
⍟	7-st nupp (see Stitch Guide)
↑	p7tog
v	sl 1 pwise wyf
▨	no stitch
▭	pattern repeat

Summer Lace Edge

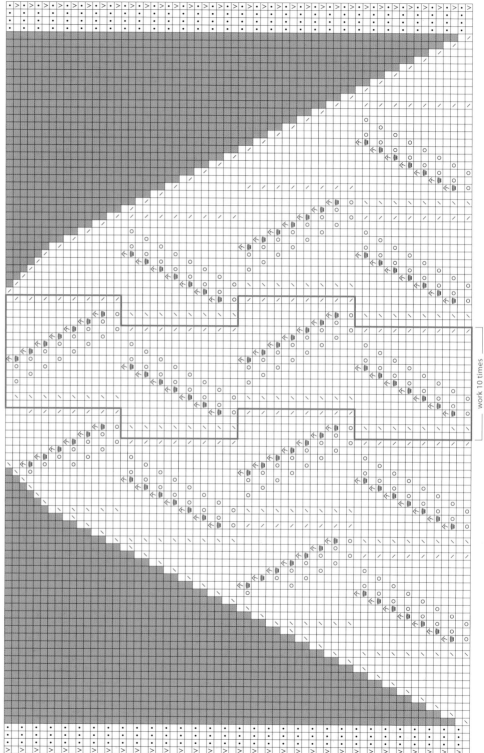

Summer Center Chart 1

	k on RS; p on WS
·	p on RS; k on WS
o	yo
/	k2tog on RS; p2tog on WS
\	sl 1, k1, psso on RS; sl 1, p1, psso on WS
⅄	sl 1, k2tog, psso
♒	7-st nupp (see Stitch Guide)
↑	p7tog
v	sl 1 pwise wyf
▓	no stitch
▢	pattern repeat

Make photo enlargements
of the charts, if desired.

Summer Center Chart 2

Summer Center Chart 3

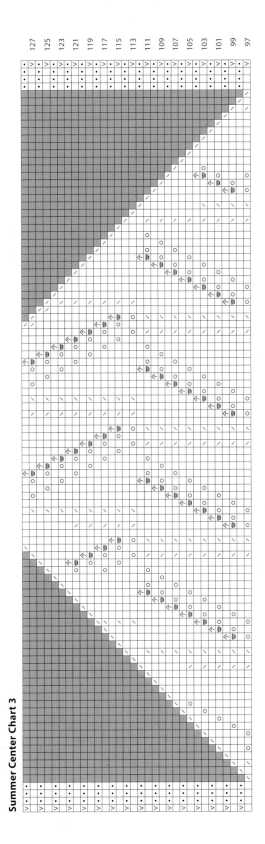

TRIANGULAR SUMMER SHAWL

LILY OF THE VALLEY SCARF

This soft and interesting-to-knit scarf was adapted from a pattern for a triangular shawl in issue #142 of *Triinu* magazine, published in the autumn of 1988. The article was written by Salme Puus, an Estonian who was living in Australia at the same time. The center of the scarf features the familiar Lily of the Valley motif, along with small flower figures that include openwork leaves and stems. The ends of the scarf have a scalloped lace borders, separated from the main section by garter-stitch bands punctuated with eyelets; the sides have narrow garter-stitch edges that prevent them from curling.

Finished Size
About 10" (25.5 cm) wide and 44" (112 cm) long, relaxed after blocking.

Yarn
Fingering weight (#1 Super Fine).
Shown here: Jojoland Cashmere 2-Ply (100% cashmere; 400 yd [366 m]/2 oz [56.7 g]): #2-101 natural brown, 1 skein (see Notes).

Needles
Size U.S. 3 (3.25 mm). Adjust needle size if necessary to obtain the correct gauge.

Notions
Markers (m); stitch holder; tapestry needle.

Gauge
10 stitches and 18 rows = 2" (5 cm) in stockinette stitch, before blocking; 20-stitch pattern repeat of Lily and Small Flower Center chart measures about 3½" (9 cm) wide, relaxed after blocking.

STITCH GUIDE

5-Stitch Nupp

Working very loosely, work (k1, yo, k1, yo, k1) all in same st—5 nupp sts made from 1 st. On the foll row, purl the 5 nupp sts tog (as shown on chart)—5 nupp sts dec'd back to 1 st.

Notes

~ The shawl is worked in one piece from the lower border to the top of the center section. The top border is worked separately so its direction of knitting will match the lower border, then the two pieces are grafted together with the Kitchener stitch.

~ A double strand of yarn is used for the cast-on, then a single strand is used for the remainder of the shawl.

~ There was very little leftover yarn after finishing the scarf shown. Plan on purchasing extra yarn if making a longer scarf.

SCARF

With double strand of yarn and using the knitted method (see page 23), CO 63 sts. Drop the extra strand and cont with a single strand only.

Lower Lace Edge

Work Rows 1–21 of Lily Lace Edge chart, slipping the first st of every row pwise with yarn in front (wyf) except for Row 1 as shown. **Next row:** (WS) Sl 1, knit to end and *at the same time* dec 5 sts evenly spaced—58 sts rem.

Center Section

Change to Lily and Small Flower Center chart and place markers (pm) after the first 4 sts and before the last 4 sts. Slipping the first st of every row and keeping rem sts outside markers in garter st, rep Rows 1–28 of chart 9 times, then work Rows 1–14 once more—266 chart rows completed. **Next row:** (RS) Sl 1, knit to end and *at the same time* inc 5 sts evenly spaced—63 sts. Slipping first st of every row, knit 3 rows. **Next row:** (RS) Sl 1, *yo, k2tog; rep from * to end. **Next row:** (WS) Sl 1, knit to end. Cut yarn, leaving a 12" (30.5 cm) tail. Place sts on holder or set aside if you have an extra set of needles to use for the top border.

Upper Lace Edge

With double strand of yarn and using the knitted method, CO 63 sts. Cut off one strand of yarn and cont with single strand only, work Rows 1–16 of Lily Lace Edge chart, slipping the first st of every row except for Row 1 as for lower border; do not work Rows 17–21. Cut yarn, leaving a 12" (30.5 cm) tail. Without working any sts, sl all sts pwise to empty needle so needle tip points to the left with RS of piece facing.

Join Center Section and Top Border

If necessary, return held center section sts to needle with RS facing and needle tip pointing to the right. Hold center section and top border tog with RS facing outwards (WS facing tog) and both needle tips pointing to the right. Thread the yarn attached to the ball on a tapestry needle and use the Kitchener st (see page 39) to graft the two pieces together, adjusting the tension of the stitches to match the tension of the knitting. Cut grafting yarn and weave in its ends, leaving 2" (5 cm) tails that will be trimmed after blocking.

FINISHING

Handwash gently in mild soap and warm water. Pin scarf out to about 12" (30.5 cm) wide and 36" (91.5 cm) long to block, pinning out each [yo, k1, yo] point in the lace edges; finished piece will narrow and lengthen to about 10" (25.5 cm) wide and 44" (112 cm) long. When dry, weave in loose ends and trim ends of grafting yarn flush with surface of scarf.

Lily and Small Flower Center

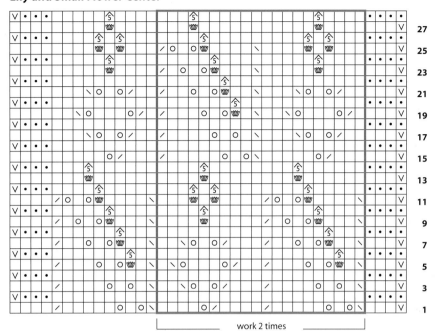

work 2 times

Lily Lace Edge

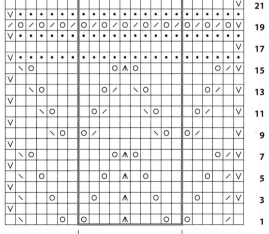

work 5 times

k on RS; p on WS

· p on RS; k on WS

o yo

∕ k2tog

＼ sl 1, k1, psso

⋏ sl 2 as if to k2tog, k1, p2sso

5-st nupp (see Stitch Guide)

p5tog

V sl 1 (see instructions)

pattern repeat

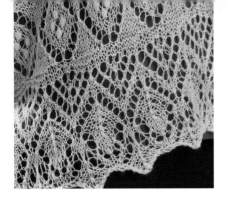

LILAC LEAF SHAWL

The center pattern for this lovely shawl is an old and very popular motif. It reminds me of the lilacs that bloom throughout Estonia in June, as well as the special lilac wood knitting needles used by the knitters of Haapsalu. This shawl begins with a lace edge I found in the book *Haapsalu Rätik*, which is followed by a diamond border pattern. The center is filled with lilac leaves and the top edge mirrors the bottom. This top edge is knitted separately and grafted onto the main piece so the direction of the knitting is the same at both ends. Garter stitches are used to visually separate the pattern motifs and provide edgings for the long sides of the shawl.

Finished Size
About 20" (51 cm) wide and 66" (167.5 cm) long, relaxed after blocking.

Yarn
Laceweight (#0 Lace).
Shown here: Wooly West Horizons Lace Yarn (100% wool; 525 yd [480 m]/50 g): natural white, 1 skein.

Needles
Size U.S. 5 (3.75 mm): straight. Adjust needle size if necessary to obtain the correct gauge.

Notions
Markers (m); stitch holder; tapestry needle.

Gauge
11 stitches and 17 rows = 2" (5 cm) in stockinette stitch, before blocking; 12-stitch pattern repeat from Lilac Leaf Center and Border chart measures about 2½" (6.5 cm) wide, relaxed after blocking.

STITCH GUIDE

7-Stitch Nupp

Working very loosely, work ([k1, yo] 3 times, k1) all in same st—7 nupp sts made from 1 st. On the foll row, purl the 7 nupp sts tog (as shown on chart)—7 nupp sts dec'd back to 1 st.

Notes

~ The shawl is worked in one piece from the lower lace edging to the top of the center section. The top lace edging is worked separately so its direction of knitting will match the lower edging, then the two pieces are grafted together with the Kitchener stitch.

~ A double strand of yarn is used for the cast-on, then a single strand is used for the remainder of the shawl.

SHAWL

Lower Lace Edging, Border, and Center

With yarn doubled and using the knitted method (see page 23), CO 95 sts. Cut off one strand of yarn and cont with a single strand only. Knit 2 rows. Work Rows 1–56 of Lilac Leaf Lace Edge and Border chart, placing markers (pm) after the first 5 sts and before the last 5 sts, slipping the first st of every row except Row 1 as if to purl with yarn in front (pwise wyf), and keeping rem sts outside markers in garter st. Change to Lilac Leaf Center and Border chart. Maintaining 5 sts at each end of needle as established, rep Rows 1–20 of chart a total

of 14 times, then work Rows 21–62 of chart once, ending with a WS row—322 rows completed from Lilac Leaf Center and Border chart; 378 chart rows completed from beg. Cut yarn, leaving a 12" (30.5 cm) tail. Place sts on holder, or set aside if you have an extra set of needles to use for the top lace edging.

Top Lace Edging

With yarn doubled and using the knitted method, CO 95 sts. Cut off one strand of yarn and cont with a single strand only. Knit 2 rows. Work only Rows 1–32 of Lilac Leaf Lace Edge and Border chart as indicated, placing markers as shown. Cut yarn, leaving a 12" (30.5 cm) tail. Without working any sts, sl all sts pwise to empty needle so needle tip points to the left with RS of piece facing.

Join Center Section to Top Lace Edging

If necessary, return held center section sts to needle with RS facing and needle tip pointing to the right. Hold center section and top lace edging tog with RS facing outwards (WS facing tog) and both needle tips pointing to the right. Thread the yarn attached to the ball on a tapestry needle and use the Kitchener st (see page 39) to graft the two pieces together, adjusting the tension of the stitches to match the tension of the knitting. Cut grafting yarn and weave in its ends, leaving 2" (5 cm) tails that will be trimmed after blocking.

FINISHING

Handwash gently in mild soap and warm water. Pin scarf out to about 22" (56 cm) wide and 72" (183 cm) long to block, pinning out each [sl 2, k1, p2sso] point in each end; finished piece will relax to about 20" (51 cm) wide and 66" (167.5 cm) long. When dry, weave in loose ends and trim ends of grafting yarn flush with surface of shawl.

Lilac Leaf Lace Edge and Border

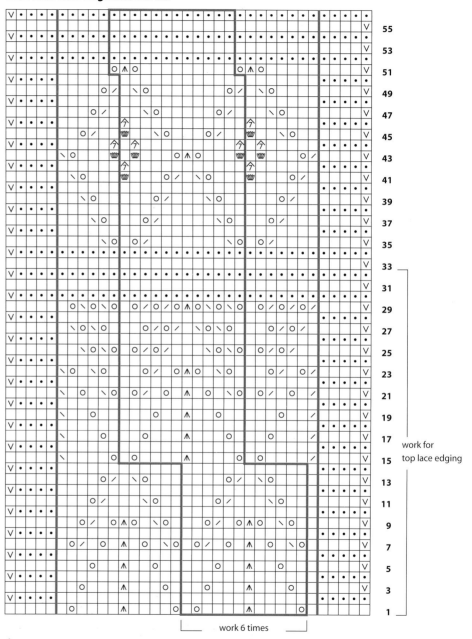

work for
top lace edging

work 6 times

KNITTED LACE OF ESTONIA

☐	**k on RS; p on WS**	
•	**p on RS; k on WS**	
o	**yo**	
/	**k2tog**	
\	**sl 1, k1, psso**	
ʌ	**sl 2 as if to k2tog, k1, p2sso**	
☟	**7-st nupp (see Stitch Guide)**	
⩘	**p7tog**	
v	**sl 1 pwise wyf (see instructions)**	
☐	**pattern repeat**	
▮	**marker position**	

Lilac Leaf Center and Border

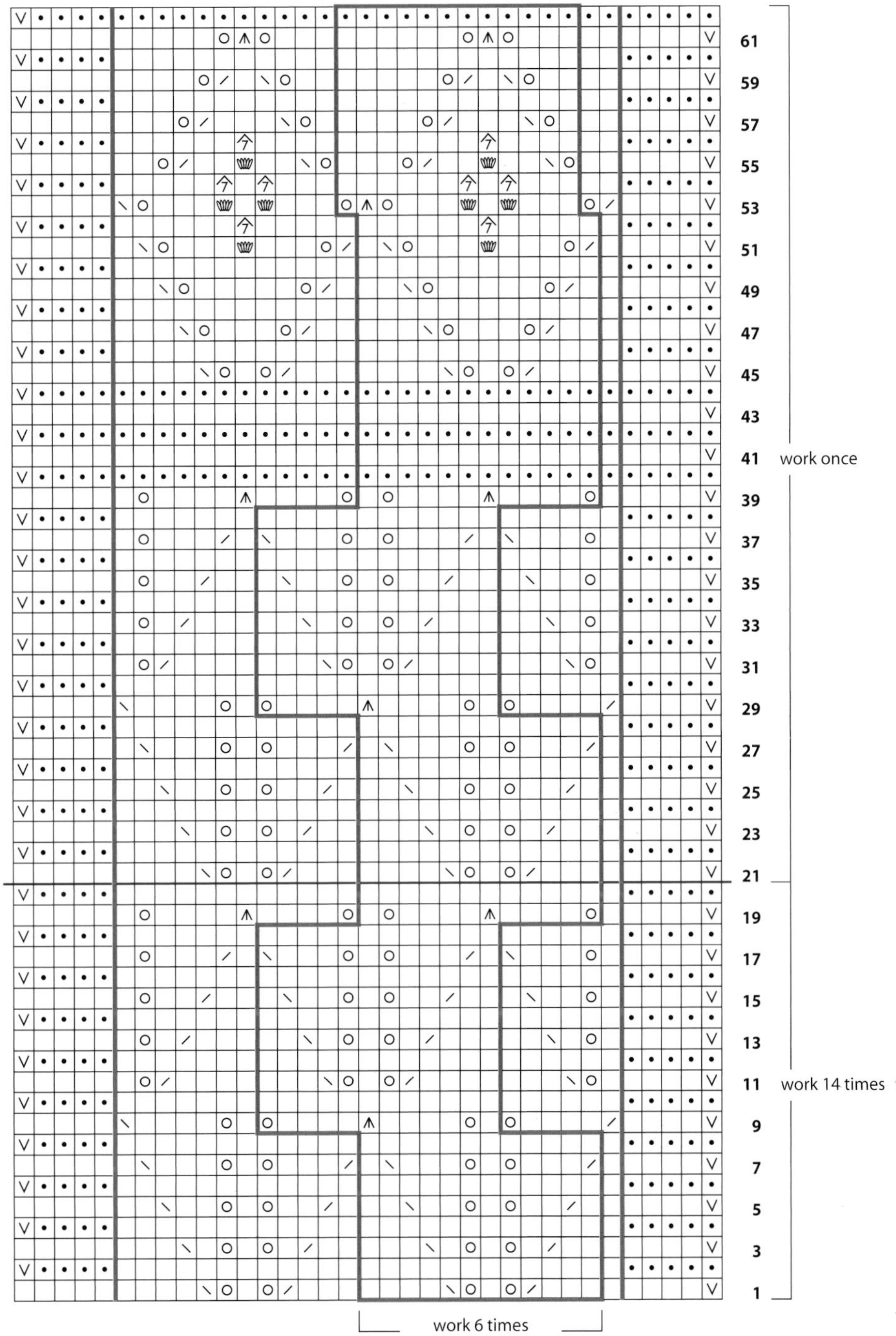

61
59
57
55
53
51
49
47
45
43
41   work once
39
37
35
33
31
29
27
25
23
21
19
17
15
13
11   work 14 times
9
7
5
3
1

work 6 times

MIRALDA'S TRIANGULAR SHAWL

This shawl was inspired by the beautiful triangular shawls being made in Haapsalu today. I was intrigued by their construction and bought several to study and decipher. In addition, Miralda Piper, one of my dear knitting friends in Haapsalu, gave me a number of traditional motifs and some helpful clues to their "secrets." The original shawls are larger, but I prefer this smaller size for wearing with a coat or jacket.

Finished Size
About 59" (150 cm) wide across top edge and 30" (76 cm) long from center of top edge to tip of lower point, relaxed after blocking.

Yarn
Fingering weight (#1 Super Fine).
Shown here: Rovings 100% Polworth 2-Ply Fingering Weight (100% Polworth wool; 820 yd [750 m]/150 g): natural sheep's gray (taupe), 1 skein.

Needles
Size U.S. 6 (4 mm): 32" (80 cm) or longer circular (cir) and 2 double-pointed (dpn). Adjust needle size if necessary to obtain the correct gauge.

Notions
Markers (m); tapestry needle; coilless safety pin or removable marker.

Gauge
10 stitches and 16 rows = 2" (5 cm) in stockinette stitch, before blocking; 20 stitches (two pattern repeats) of Miralda Lace Edge charts measure about 5" (12.5 cm) wide, relaxed after blocking; 20-stitch pattern repeat of Diamond charts measures about 5" (12.5 cm) wide, relaxed after blocking.

STITCH GUIDE

5-Stitch Nupp

Working very loosely, work (k1, yo, k1, yo, k1) all in same st—5 nupp sts made from 1 st. On the foll row, purl the 5 nupp sts tog (as shown on chart)—5 nupp sts dec'd back to 1 st.

Gathered Sts (worked over 3 sts)

K3tog but do not slip sts from needle, yo, then knit the same 3 sts tog again, then slip all 3 sts from needle.

3-Stitch Cross (worked over 3 sts)

Sl 1 st as if to purl with yarn in back, knit the next 2 sts, then pass the slipped st over the 2 sts just knitted—3 sts dec'd to 2 sts. On the foll WS row, work a yo between the 2 resulting sts as shown on charts, to inc to 3 sts again.

Note

~ The scarf begins with stitches cast on for the lace edge along the two lower sides, then stitches are decreased to produce a triangle shape. When only the stitches of the garter edgings remain, these stitches are grafted or bound off together at the center of the top edge to finish the scarf.

SCARF

With yarn doubled and using the knitted method (see page 23), CO 331 sts. Cut off one strand of yarn and cont with a single strand only. Knit 2 rows.

Lace Edge

Set up patt for lace edge charts as foll: Work Row 1 of Miralda Right Lace Edge chart across first 166 sts, placing a marker (pm) after the first 4 sts, then work Row 1 of Miralda Left Lace Edge chart over 165 sts, pm before last 4 sts—329 sts. Place a removable marker in the center st itself (shown in gold) and not on the needle, and move this marker up every few rows so you can always easily identify the center st. Work Rows 2–20 of Right and Left Lace Edge charts as established—305 sts.

Border

Change to Miralda Lower Border chart and work Rows 1–12—281 sts. Set up patt for diamond charts as foll: Work Row 1 of Miralda Right Diamond chart across first 141 sts, then work Row 1 of Miralda Left Diamond chart across last 140 sts. Work Rows 2–34 of Right and Left Diamond charts as established—213 sts. Change to Miralda Upper Border chart and work Rows 1–14—185 sts.

Center Section

Set up patt for center charts as foll: Work Row 1 of Miralda Right Center chart across first 93 sts, then work Row 1 of Miralda Left Center chart across last 92 sts. Work Rows 2–24 of charts once, then rep Rows 1–24 two more times—41 sts rem. **Note:** The first time you work Rows 1–24, work each marked 4-st section 13 times; the second time you work Rows 1–24, work each marked 4-st section 7 times; the third time you work Rows 1–24, work each marked 4-st section only once. Work Rows 25–38 of charts and on Rows 35 and 37 dec only in the center as shown; do not dec inside the markers at each side—17 sts rem: 1 center st plus 8 garter edging sts at each side. **Next row:** (WS) K2tog, yo, k6, k2tog, k7—16 sts rem. Arrange sts

evenly on 2 dpn so there are 8 sts on each needle. Cut yarn, leaving a 12" (30.5 cm) tail. Thread the tail on a tapestry needle, hold the dpn with RS facing outward (WS facing tog) and use the Kitchener stitch (see page 39) to graft the sts tog. For an optional non-grafted finish, hold the dpn with WS facing outward (RS facing tog) and use the empty cir needle to join sts using the three-needle bind-off method (see page 38).

FINISHING

Handwash gently in mild soap and warm water. Pin shawl out to about 64" (162.5 cm) wide across top edge and 31" (78.5 cm) from center of top edge to tip of lower point, pinning out each [sl 2, k1, p2sso] point along the lace edges; finished piece will relax to about 59" (150 cm) wide across the top and 30" (76 cm) long. When dry, weave in loose ends.

☐	k on RS; p on WS
•	p on RS; k on WS
○	yo
╱	k2tog
╲	sl 1, k1, psso
⋀	sl 2 as if to k2tog, k1, p2sso
♨	5-st nupp (see Stitch Guide)
⬆	p5tog
▨	no stitch
▦	center stitch
☐	pattern repeat
❘	marker position
▷	gathered sts (see Stitch Guide)
◥	3-st cross (see Stitch Guide)

Miralda Left Lace Edge

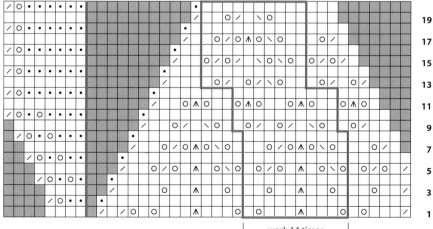

└ work 14 times ┘

Miralda Lower Border

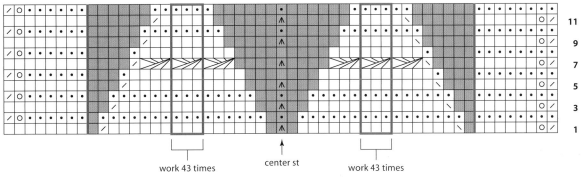

work 43 times center st work 43 times

11
9
7
5
3
1

Miralda Upper Border

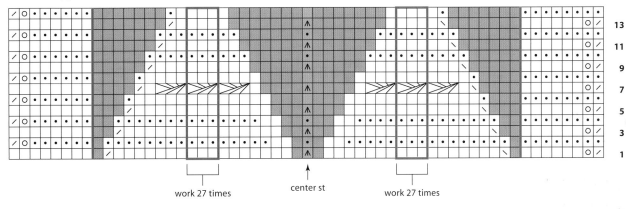

work 27 times center st work 27 times

13
11
9
7
5
3
1

Miralda Right Lace Edge

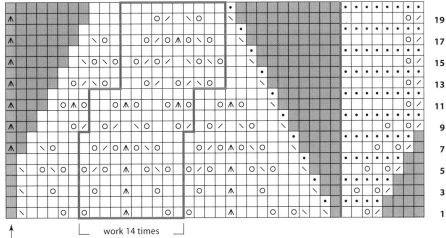

work 14 times

center st

19
17
15
13
11
9
7
5
3
1

Miralda Left Diamond

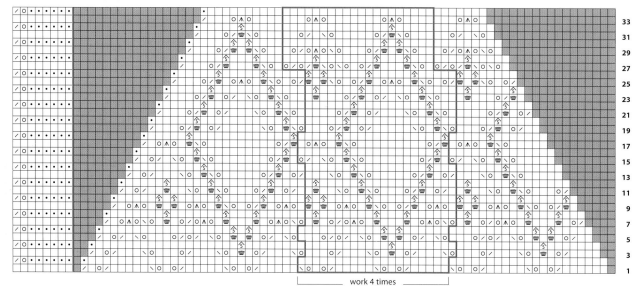

work 4 times

☐	k on RS; p on WS
·	p on RS; k on WS
○	yo
╱	k2tog
╲	sl 1, k1, psso
⋀	sl 2 as if to k2tog, k1, p2sso
♔	5-st nupp (see Stitch Guide)
⬆	p5tog
▨	no stitch
▨	center stitch
☐	pattern repeat
▮	marker position
⧄	gathered sts (see Stitch Guide)
⧄	3-st cross (see Stitch Guide)

Miralda Left Center

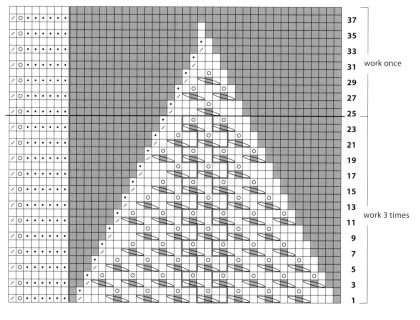

work once

work 3 times

Miralda Right Diamond

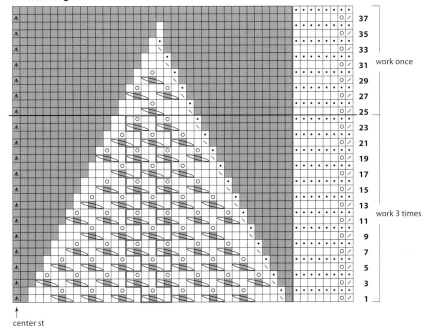

work 4 times

↑ center st

Miralda Right Center

work once

work 3 times

↑ center st

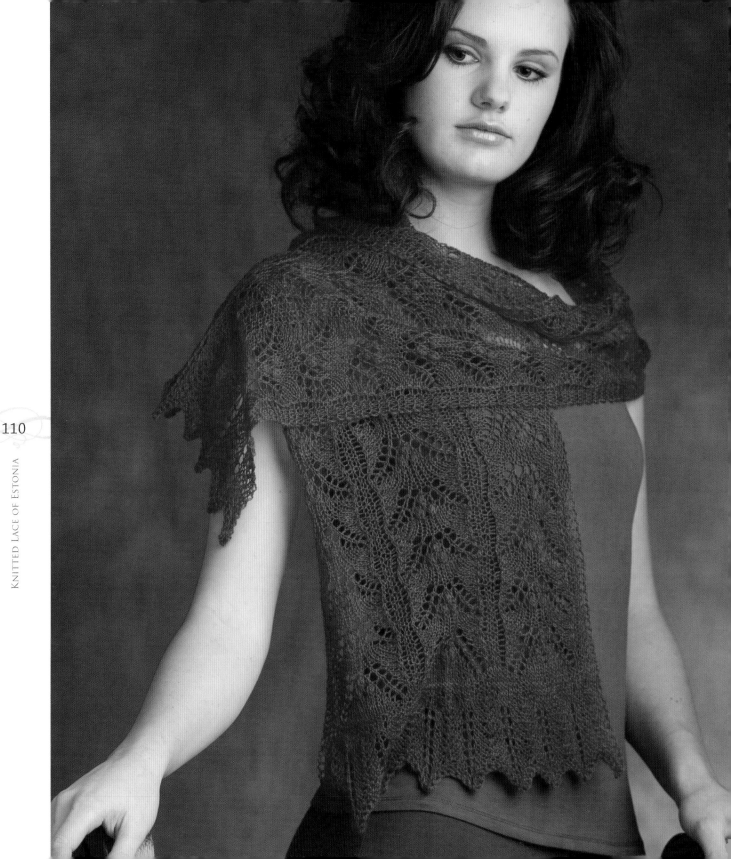

TRIINU SCARF

This scarf pattern was inspired by an article written by Ülle Slamer in issue #148, *Kevad* (Spring) 1990 of *Triinu* magazine. According to the article translated by Helle-Mall, "The original shawl came as a present from Estonia. Although we had a few members in our crafts group who had knitted many shawls, nobody had seen this pattern before. So, we gave the shawl to Helle-Mall Risti who worked out the pattern and put it on paper so that it could be easily followed. At the next teaching workshop, most chose to use this pattern. The results were very interesting as the size of the shawl depended on the wool used. Also wool in different colors was used including the traditional white. The exhibition in September 1989 was very impressive with so many fine shawls hanging on the stands."

Finished Size
About 11" (28 cm) wide and 63" (160 cm) long, after blocking.

Yarn
Fingering weight (#1 Super Fine).
Shown here: Shelridge Farm Soft Touch Lace, (100% wool; 500 yd [455 m]/50 g): Rust, 1 skein.

Needles
Size U.S. 4 (3.5 mm). Adjust needle size if necessary to obtain the correct gauge.

Notions
Smooth cotton waste yarn, size G/6 (4.25 mm) crochet hook; markers (m); tapestry needle.

Gauge
11½ stitches and 22 rows = 2" (5 cm) in stockinette stitch, before blocking; 21-stitch pattern repeat of Trinu Center chart measures about 3¼" (8.5 cm) wide, after blocking.

STITCH GUIDE

7-Stitch Nupp

Working very loosely, work ([k1, yo] 3 times, k1) all in same st—7 nupp sts made from 1 st. On the foll row, purl the 7 nupp sts tog (as shown on chart)—7 nupp sts dec'd back to 1 st.

SCARF

With cotton waste yarn and crochet hook, chain about 75 sts (see page 37). Tie a knot in the end of the cotton after the last chain to identify this end later. With needles and working yarn, pick up and knit 69 sts from the center 69 "bumps" along the back of the crochet chain. Beg and end with a RS row, work 3 rows of garter st, knitting the first st of the first row, but slipping the first st of every row thereafter pwise with yarn in front (wyf). **Next row:** (WS) Sl 1, purl to end. Change to Triinu Center chart and place markers (pm) after the first 4 sts and before the last 4 sts. Slipping the first st of every row and keeping rem sts outside markers in garter st as shown, rep Rows 1–12 twenty-nine times, or until piece measures about 6½" (16.5 cm) less than desired total length—348 chart rows completed. Slipping the first st of every row, knit 6 rows and *at the same time* inc 22 sts evenly spaced on the last WS row—91 sts. Knit 1 RS row, then purl 1 WS row.

Top Lace Edge

Work Rows 1–17 of Triinu Lace Edge chart. **Note:** First st of every row is not slipped for lace edge. With yarn doubled, BO all sts on next WS row. Break yarn, leaving a 6" (15 cm) tail.

Bottom Lace Edge

Beg at knotted end, carefully remove the waste-yarn crochet chain, placing each live st on needle as it becomes free—69 sts. If necessary, re-orient the sts on the needle so RS of scarf is facing you, and join yarn ready to work a RS row. Knit 2 rows and *at the same time* inc 22 sts evenly spaced on second row—91 sts. Knit 1 RS row, then purl WS 1 row. Work Rows 1–17 of Triinu Lace Edge chart as for top lace edge. With yarn doubled, BO all sts on next WS row. Break yarn, leaving a 6" (15 cm) tail.

FINISHING

Handwash gently with mild soap and warm water. Pin scarf out to desired measurements, pinning out each [yo, k1, yo] point in the lace edges. When dry, weave in loose ends.

Triinu Lace Edge

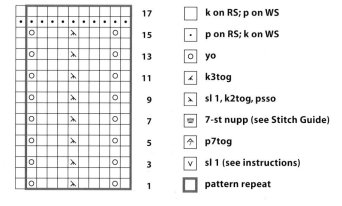

□	k on RS; p on WS
·	p on RS; k on WS
o	yo
⋏	k3tog
⅄	sl 1, k2tog, psso
♕	7-st nupp (see Stitch Guide)
↑	p7tog
v	sl 1 (see instructions)
□	pattern repeat

Triinu Center

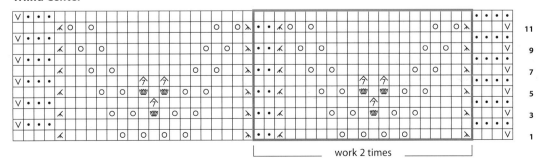

work 2 times

CROWN PRINCE SQUARE SHAWL

This lovely square shawl pattern comes from the *Talv* (Winter) 1981 issue #115 of *Triinu* magazine. The article was written by Helve Poska. Although the published pattern is not a duplication of the original given to Swedish Crown Prince Gustav–Adolf in 1936, the pattern was charted from a photograph of a similar shawl knitted by Matilde Möll. This pattern was designed by Möll's mother, Mrs. Valdman, who knitted the original shawl for the Crown Prince. The shawl photographed in the Triinu article was knitted by Loora Kurba at the *Haapsalu Räätikute* (Haapsalu shawl) workshop of the Estonian Ethnographical Club in Stockholm, Sweden. Following Helle-Mall Risti's suggestion, this version has 24 stitches (two pattern repeats) added to each lace edge piece to give the edge more stretch.

Finished Size
About 52" (132 cm) square, relaxed after blocking.

Yarn
Laceweight (#0 Lace).
Shown here: Skacel Merino Lace (100% merino wool; 1375 yd [1257 m]/100 g): #426 natural white, 2 skeins.

Needles
Size U.S. 4 (3.5 mm). Adjust needle size if necessary to obtain the correct gauge.

Notions
Markers (m); removable marker or safety pin; tapestry needle.

Gauge
10 stitches and 18 rows = 2" (5 cm) in stockinette stitch, before blocking; 20-stitch pattern repeat from Crown Prince Top and Bottom Border chart measures about 5½" (14 cm) wide, relaxed after blocking; 12-stitch pattern repeat from Crown Prince Center chart measures about 3¼" (8.5 cm) wide, relaxed after blocking.

Reminiscences from Helve Poska

"My grandmother Lovisa Saarek (mother's side) lived a ten-minute walk from my parents' house on Opetaja tanav (in Haapsalu) in a small house with four rooms and a large kitchen and a good-size garden. She had four kinds of apple trees, large and small plum trees, redcurrant bushes, and various other berry bushes, and she grew different vegetables and strawberries. Two of the rooms were nearly always rented out. In the winter they were let to school children from the countryside and in the summer there were summer guests living there, often the same family for several summers in a row. Grandma always sat in her room by a table with a white tablecloth by a window filled with flowerpots. She loved begonias. My grandma taught me to knit when I was only four years old. I knitted little shawls to my dolls and she knitted large square ones with border lace or with long tassels. She knitted her shawls to be sold to a buyer from Tallinn who sent them on to the U.S.A. I liked watching her and smelling the scent of wet wool shawls when they were assembled onto frames to dry. Afterwards they were stiff. I loved my grandma and she loved me and my siblings. My mother was an only child. When my grandmother died in 1941 (during the war) I decided to become a handicraft/sewing teacher. I traveled to Tallinn and studied two years at a handicraft college after which I returned to Haapsalu to practice as a teacher. I was only 18 years old. When I was 19, I came to Sweden where I demonstrated for the first time in 1947 how to knit a Haapsalu ratik. Since then I have given several courses and been to many exhibitions. I worked as an office clerk doing book-keeping. I was never good at knitting but enjoyed making patterns and descriptions, knitting different pattern samples, and teaching knitting Haapsalu rätikud. I only taught patterns from before the second World War."

STITCH GUIDE

7-Stitch Nupp

Working very loosely, work ([k1, yo] 3 times, k1) all in same st—7 nupp sts made from 1 st. On the foll row, purl the 7 nupp sts tog (as shown on chart)—7 nupp sts dec'd back to 1 st.

Notes

~ The center square of the shawl is worked in one piece. The lace edge is worked in two identical pieces that are sewn to the center section.

~ Unless otherwise instructed, work the first 7 stitches of every row of center square as slip 1 as if to purl with yarn in front (pwise wyf), k6; then work the last 7 stitches of every row of shawl center as k7.

CENTER SQUARE

Using the knitted method (see page 23), CO 153 sts. **Next row:** (RS) Knit. **Next row:** (WS) Sl 1 (see Notes), knit to end. Rep the last row 12 more times—14 garter st rows completed. **Next row:** (RS) Sl 1, k6, place marker (pm), k139, pm, k7. **Next row:** (WS) Sl 1 pwise wyf, k6, purl to last 7 sts, k7. Establish patt from Crown Prince Top and Bottom Border chart on next RS row as foll: Work 7 sts before marker (m) as established, work Row 1 of chart over center 139 sts, work 7 sts after m as established. Cont to work edgings outside m as established, work Rows 2–34 of chart. Establish patts from Crown Prince Side Border and Center charts on next RS row as foll: Work first 7 sts as established, work Row 1 of Crown Prince Side Border chart over next 19 sts, pm, work Row 1 of Crown Prince Center chart over next 101 sts, pm, work Row 1 of Crown Prince Side Border chart over next 19 sts, work last 7 sts as established. On the

foll rows, for Side Border chart work Rows 2–40 once, then work Rows 1–40 four times, then work Rows 1–6 once more; for Center chart work Rows 2–28 once, work Rows 29–52 six times, then work Rows 53–86 once—206 patt rows total from beg of Side Border and Center charts. Change to Crown Prince Top and Bottom Border chart and, working 7 sts at each side as established, work Rows 1–34 of chart. **Next row:** (RS) Sl 1, knit to end. **Next row:** (WS) Sl 1, k6, purl to last 7 sts, k7. Slipping first st of each row as established, work 13 rows in garter st, beg and ending with a RS row. With WS facing and using the k2tog method (see page 27), loosely BO all sts.

LACE EDGE (MAKE 2)

With yarn doubled and using the knitted method, CO 409 sts. Cut off one strand of yarn and cont with a single strand only. Knit 2 rows. Place a removable marker or safety pin on the right side of the piece. Work Rows 1–21 of Crown Prince Lace Edge chart; do not slip the first st of each row. With WS facing and using the k2tog method, loosely BO all sts. Make a second lace edge the same as the first.

Join Lace Edge to Center

Hold the center section and one lace edge with RS tog and so that the center piece is closest to you. Beg at the lower left corner (the left edge of the CO row), distribute the lace edge so that you beg with a "half point," have 16 points from the edge along one side, and the point of the 17th scallop even with the corner of the center section. With the yarn from the ball threaded on a tapestry needle, sew the two pieces tog (see page 30) as foll: Bring the threaded needle from back to front through each of the first 3 loops of the lace edge, then through the first loop of the center piece from front to back. Rep this 3:1 ratio 2 more times (3 times total)—9 sts of lace edge and

3 sts of center section have been joined. Next, take 2 loops from the lace edge and 1 loop from the center piece. Rep this 2:1 ratio 2 more times (3 times total). Work along the side of the shawl by taking 1 loop from the lace edge and 1 loop from the center 3 times, then 2 loops from the lace edge and 1 loop from the center once (i.e., 1:1, 1:1, 1:1, 2:1) until 15 sts rem before the center of the 17th scallop on the lace edge and 6 sts rem before the next corner on the center section. Next, take 2 loops from the lace edge and 1 loop from the center (2:1) 3 times, then take 3 loops from the lace edge and 1 loop from the center (3:1) 3 times, ending at the center of 17th scallop on the lace edge and the corner of the center piece. **Note:** You may need to make small adjustments (by taking more or fewer sts along the lace edge; do not skip sts on either piece or holes will form) in the sewing to end up exactly at the center of a scallop of the lace edge and the corner of the center section. Cont this process across the top of the shawl: work the 3:1 ratio 3 times, then the 2:1 ratio 3 times, then the (1:1, 1:1, 1:1, 2:1) ratio until 15 sts rem from the center of the scallop that will form the next corner and 6 sts rem before the corner of the center section. Then, work the 2:1 ratio 3 times, then the 3:1 ratio 3 times to end up at the corner.

Join the other lace edge to the rem 2 sides of the center section in the same manner, beg along the side and ending across the bottom of the shawl. Using a tail from the center section or separate length of yarn, sew the lace edgings tog at the corners. Check to make sure there are no puckers or tight areas in the seam before cutting the seaming yarn.

FINISHING

Handwash gently with mild soap and warm water. Pin shawl out to about 54" (137 cm) square, pinning out each [sl 1, k2tog, psso] point along the lace edge; finished piece will relax to about 54" (137 cm) square. When dry, weave in loose ends.

Crown Prince Top and Bottom Border

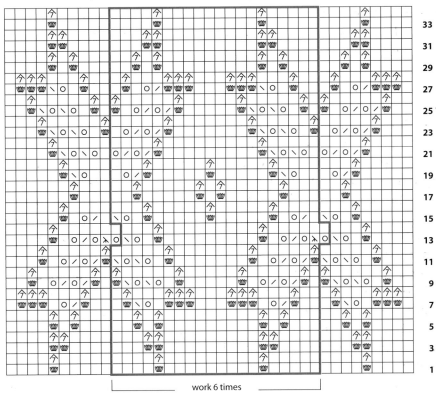

work 6 times

Crown Prince Lace Edge

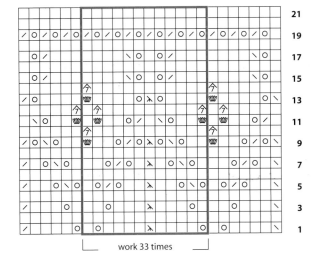

work 33 times

	k on RS; p on WS
•	p on RS; k on WS
O	yo
/	k2tog
\	sl 1, k1, psso
⋏	sl 1, k2tog, psso
♛	7-st nupp (see Stitch Guide)
⌃	p7tog
▢	pattern repeat

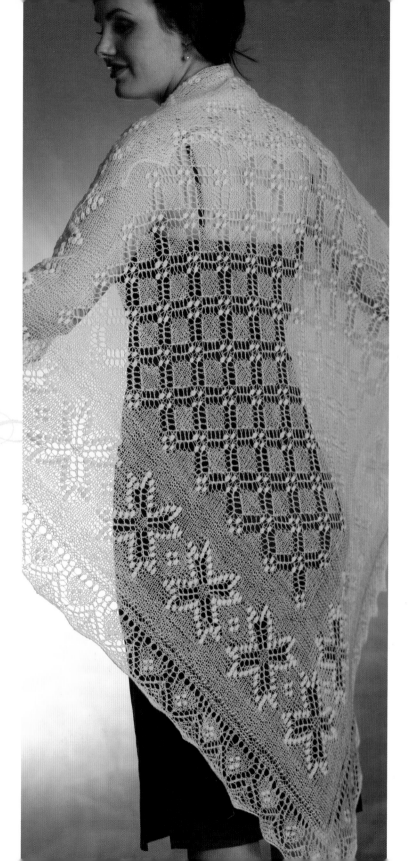

Crown Prince Side Border

	39
	37
	35
	33
	31
	29
	27
	25
	23
	21
	19
	17
	15
	13
	11
	9
	7
	5
	3
	1

Crown Prince Center

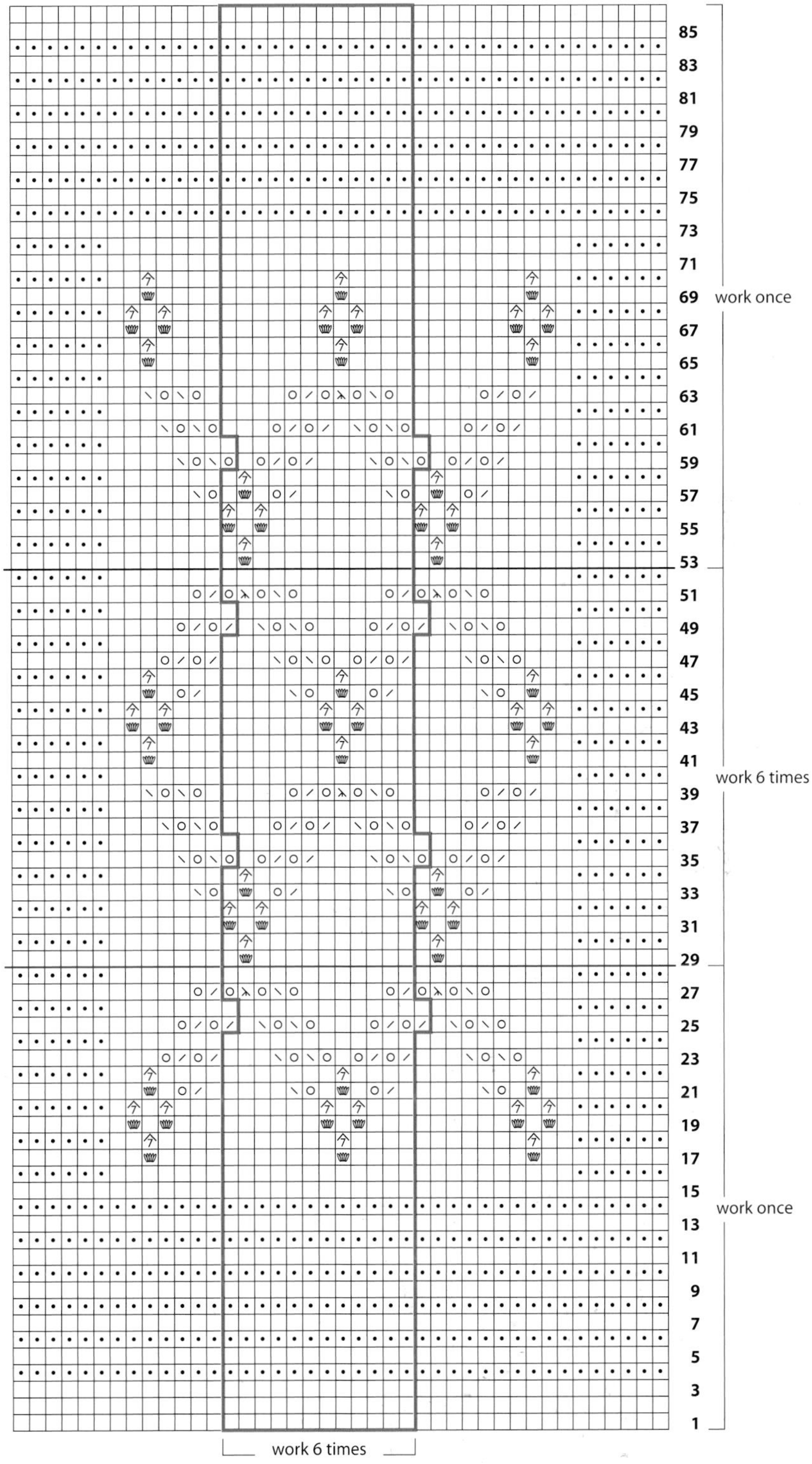

work once

work 6 times

work once

work 6 times

Legend:

- ☐ k on RS; p on WS
- • p on RS; k on WS
- ○ yo
- ╱ k2tog
- ╲ sl 1, k1, psso
- ⋋ sl 1, k2tog, psso
- ♛ 7-st nupp (see Stitch Guide)
- ↑ p7tog
- ▢ pattern repeat

Row numbers (right side): 1, 3, 5, 7, 9, 11, 13, 15, 17, 19, 21, 23, 25, 27, 29, 31, 33, 35, 37, 39, 41, 43, 45, 47, 49, 51, 53, 55, 57, 59, 61, 63, 65, 67, 69, 71, 73, 75, 77, 79, 81, 83, 85

ESTONIAN LACE STITCH DICTIONARY

When planning this dictionary to supplement the lace patterns in the projects, I collected the most classic and traditional Estonian lace patterns I could find and those that had been named or could easily be named. As a collection, these patterns represent the variety of patterns developed and loved by Estonian lace knitters.

These patterns come from a number of sources. Many were handwritten on graph paper for me by knitters in Haapsalu. Some came from various volumes of *Triinu* magazine, published from 1951 to 1995. Many of the patterns were popular before WW II. Others came from the booklet *Haapsalu Rätik* published by the Federated Estonian Woman's Clubs in New York in 1972. Still others are from the three editions of Leili (Lehismets) Reimann's book *Pitsilised Koekirjad* (Lace Knitting Patterns), published in 1978, 1986, and 1995, with some additions and variations included in each edition. These books contain many lace patterns, not only patterns acceptable for Estonian lace shawls, but for lace knitting in general, collected from different sources and some created by Reimann herself. These books, in Estonian, are a source for ideas as well as information about modern shawl construction.

In the limited space available, I've included patterns that can be used for the center section of shawls and scarves. There are a variety of beloved leaf and Lily of the Valley patterns, patterns featuring motifs inspired by nature and everyday life, and patterns designed specifically to honor Greta Garbo and the Crown Prince of Sweden. There are also two border patterns that can be used as a frame around the center section of square shawls, and edge patterns that can be used to finish a shawl or scarf with a classic lacy scalloped edge, whether sewn on in the traditional method or picked up and knitted in the modern method.

In some cases the original charts have been reworked to make the patterns easier to follow than they might otherwise have been. Often, one repeat of the pattern was all that was available to me, either written out in Estonian words or charted. When space allows, the charts here provide a bigger picture of the motifs to show how they look when repeated in width and height.

The symbols used for nupps on the charts don't specify the exact number of stitches to work. This number depends on the weight of the yarn. In general, five stitches are used with thick yarns; seven or nine stitches are used with thinner yarns. Knit a swatch to determine the number that you like best with your yarn.

STITCH GUIDE

Increase 1 Stitch to 3 Stitches

Knit the next st but do not slip it from the left needle, yo on right needle, knit into the same st on the left needle again, slip the st off the left needle—1 st inc'd to 3 sts.

5-Stitch Nupp

Working very loosely, work ([k1, yo] 2 times, k1) all in the same st—5 nupp sts made from 1 st. On the foll row, purl the 5 nupp sts tog (see page 24)—5 nupp sts dec'd back to 1 st.

7-Stitch Nupp

Working very loosely, work ([k1, yo] 3 times, k1) all in the same st—7 nupp sts made from 1 st. On the foll row, purl the 7 nupp sts tog (see page 24)—7 nupp sts dec'd back to 1 st.

3 Gathered Stitches (worked over 3 sts)

K3tog but do not slip these sts from the left needle, yo, then knit the same 3 sts tog again, then slip all 3 sts from left needle (see page 26). Be sure to work these stitches in the correct order on the following row.

5 Gathered Stitches (worked over 5 sts)

K5tog but do not slip these sts from the left needle, [yo, knit the same 5 sts tog again and leave on needle as before] 2 times, then slip all 5 sts from left needle (see page 27). Be sure to work these stitches in the correct order on the following row.

□	k on RS; p on WS
·	p on RS; k on WS
o	yo
/	k2tog
\	sl 1, k1, psso
⅄	p2tog
⅄	sl 1, p1, psso
⋌	k3tog
x	p3tog
⅄	sl 1, k2tog, psso
∧	sl 2 as if to k2tog, k1, p2sso
⬇	inc 1 st to 3 sts (see Stitch Guide)
♛	nupp (see Notes)
⬆	purl all nupp sts tog (# = number of sts in nupp)
■	corner stitch
▦	no stitch
□	pattern repeat
▷▷	3 gathered sts (see Stitch Guide)
▷▷	5 gathered sts (see Stitch Guide)
⋈	sl 3 sts onto cn, hold in back, k3, k3 from cn
⋈	sl 3 sts onto cn, hold in front, k3, k3 from cn

LEAF AND TWIG PATTERNS

Lehekiri (Leaf Pattern)

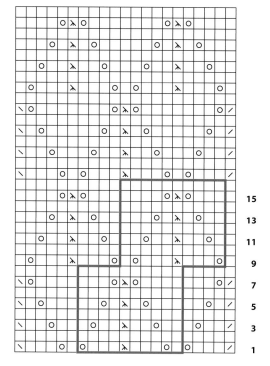

pattern repeat:
multiple of 10 sts + 11; 16 rows

source: *Haapsalu Rätik*, New York, 1972

See page 123 for chart symbols.

Poollehekiri (Half Leaf Pattern)

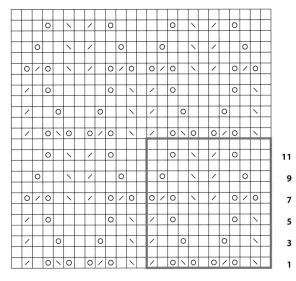

11
9
7
5
3
1

pattern repeat:
multiple of 12 sts + 13; 12 rows

source: *Haapsalu Rätik*, New York, 1972

Viislehekiri (Five Leaf Pattern)

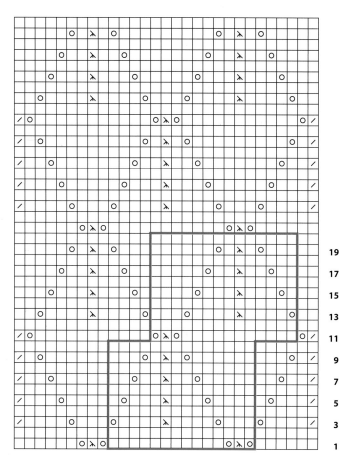

pattern repeat:
multiple of 14 sts + 15; 20 rows

source: *Triinu* #111, 1980

See page 123 for chart symbols.

Saarelehekiri (Ash Leaf Pattern)

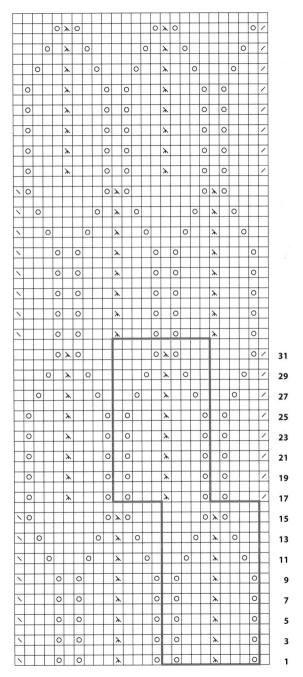

pattern repeat:
multiple of 10 sts + 6; 32 rows

source: *Triinu* #111, 1980

Kaselehekiri (Birch Leaf Pattern)

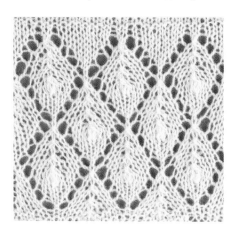

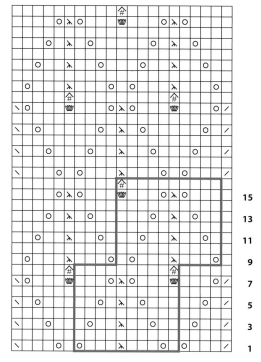

pattern repeat:
multiple of 10 sts + 11; 16 rows

source: *Triinu* #111, 1980

See page 123 for chart symbols.

Hagakiri (Twig Pattern)

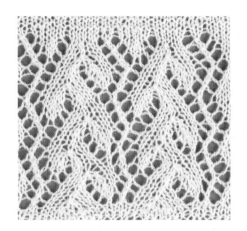

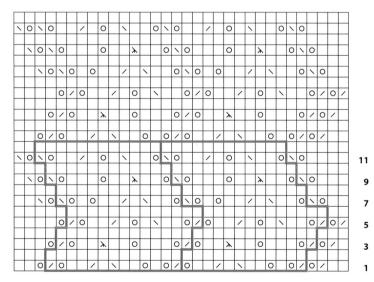

Row numbers on right: 11, 9, 7, 5, 3, 1

pattern repeat:
multiple of 12 sts + 8; 12 rows

source: from Haapsalu, handwritten

Hagakiri 2 (Twig Pattern 2)

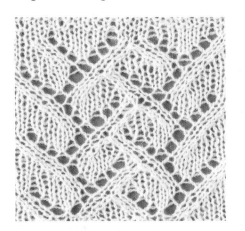

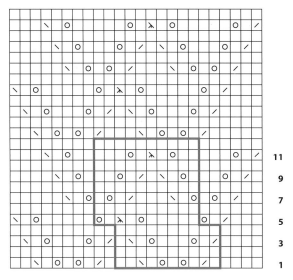

pattern repeat:
multiple of 10 sts + 14; 12 rows

sources: *Triinu* #111, 1980;
Haapsalu Rätik, New York, 1972

See page 123 for chart symbols.

Kahekordne Hagakiri (Double Twig Pattern)

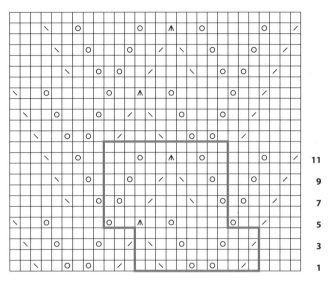

pattern repeat:
multiple of 12 sts + 16; 12 rows

source: *Triinu* #111, 1980

LILY OF THE VALLEY PATTERNS

**Ühekordse Maikellukese Kiri
(Single Lily of the Valley Pattern)**

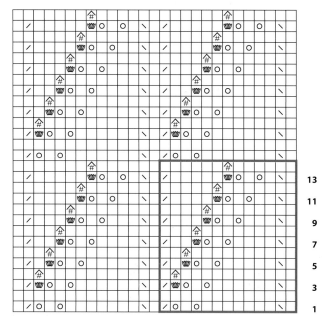

pattern repeat:
multiple of 13 sts + 1; 14 rows

sources: *Triinu* #111, 1980;
Haapsalu Rätik, New York, 1972

See page 123 for chart symbols.

Kahekordse Maikellukese Kiri
(Double Lily of the Valley Pattern)

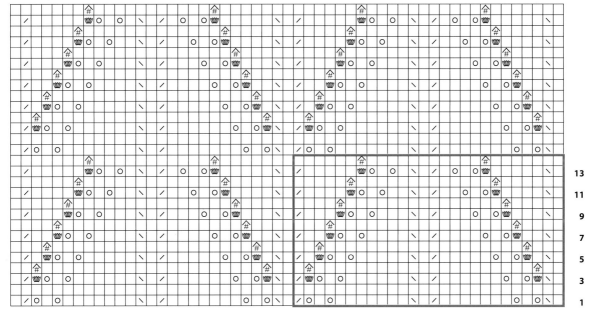

pattern repeat:
multiple of 26 sts + 1; 14 rows

sources: *Triinu* #111, 1980;
Haapsalu Rätik, New York, 1972

Maikellukese Kiri 1
(Lily of the Valley Pattern 1)

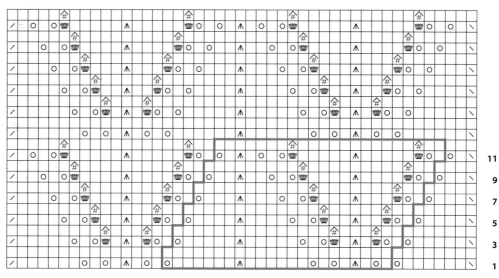

pattern repeat:
multiple of 22 sts + 23; 12 rows

source: *Triinu* #113, 1981

See page 123 for chart symbols.

Maikellukese Kiri 2
(Lily of the Valley Pattern 2)

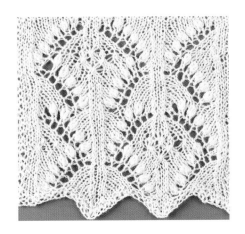

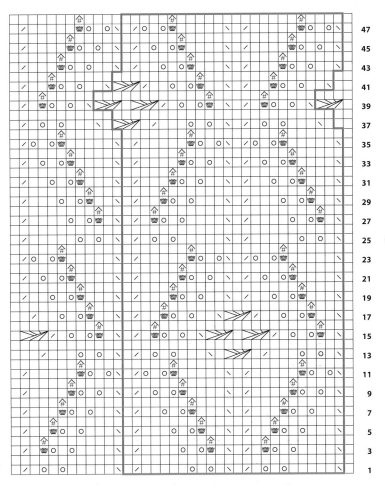

pattern repeat:
multiple of 24 sts + 13; 48 rows

source: *Triinu* #113, 1981

Piibelehtkiri (Lily of the Valley Pattern)

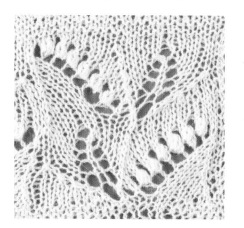

27
25
23
21
19
17
15
13
11
9
7
5
3
1

pattern repeat:
multiple of 21 sts + 11; 28 rows

source: Haapsalu, handwritten,
design attributed to Ester Niip

See page 123 for chart symbols.

Piibelehtkiri is another word for lily of the valley. This is a modern design from Haapsalu. A shawl done in this pattern was given to Ingrid Rüütel, the former First Lady of Estonia by the knitters of Haapsalu. Ingrid Rüütel is also an ethnographer and is involved in preserving Estonia's folk traditions.

Other Nature and Domestic Patterns

Mustikakiri (Blueberry Pattern)

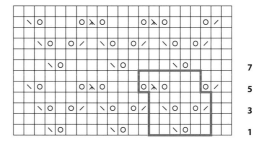

3

1

pattern repeat:
multiple of 4 sts; 4 rows

source: *Pitsilised Koekirjad*
by Leili Reimann
Valgus, 1986, Tallinn, Estonia
pattern #20, pages 42 and 134

Kalasabakiri (Fishtail Pattern)

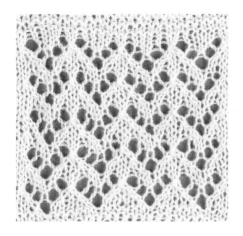

7

5

3

1

pattern repeat:
multiple of 6 sts + 9; 6 rows

source: *Haapsalu Rätik*, New York, 1972

Lepatrinukiri (Ladybug Pattern)

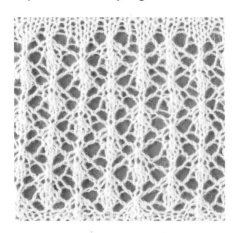

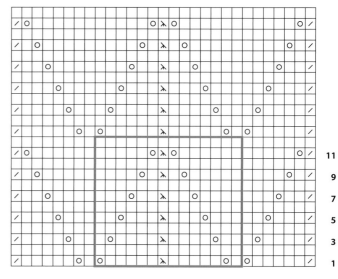

pattern repeat:
multiple of 6 sts + 7; 8 rows

source: *Haapsalu Rätik*, New York, 1972

Vausabakiri (Peacock Tail Pattern)

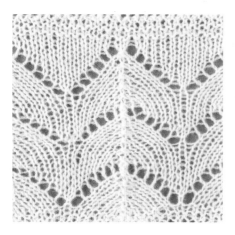

See page 123 for chart symbols.

pattern repeat:
multiple of 14 sts + 15; 12 rows

source: *Triinu* #111, 1980

KNITTED LACE OF ESTONIA

Pohlamarjakiri (Ligonberry Pattern)

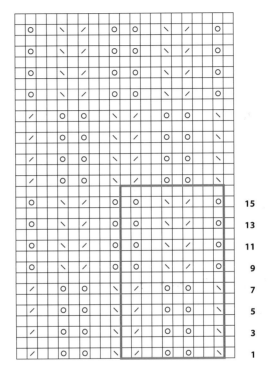

pattern repeat:
multiple of 10 sts + 1; 16 rows

source: *Haapsalu Rätik*, New York, 1972

Liblikakiri (Butterfly Pattern)

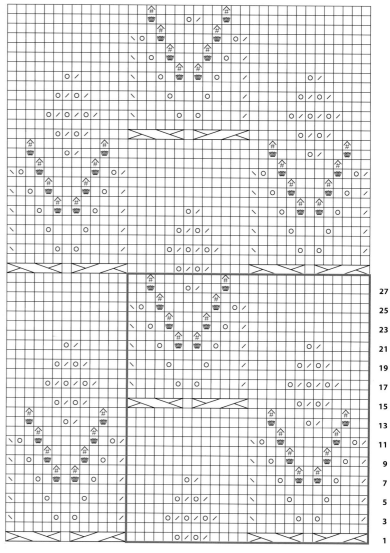

See page 123 for chart symbols.

pattern repeat:
multiple of 26 sts or 26 sts + 13; 28 rows

source: Haapsalu, handwritten

Repeat only the marked 26-stitch pattern for an allover design or work
in multiples of 26 stitches plus the extra 13 stitches to balance the pattern.

Präänikukiri (Präänick Pattern)

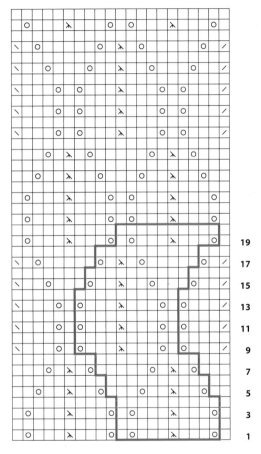

19
17
15
13
11
9
7
5
3
1

pattern repeat:
multiple of 10 sts + 11; 20 rows

source: Haapsalu, handwritten

Präänik is a type of cookie. This pattern is one
of the oldest, according to the ladies in Haapsalu.
Children used to start with this pattern because
it was easy to teach and to learn. "More experienced"
knitters in Haapsalu usually don't knit this pattern.

Tapeetkiri (Wallpaper Pattern)

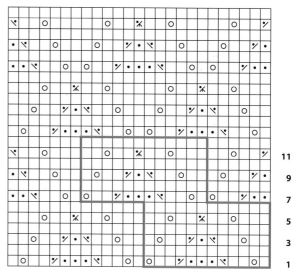

pattern repeat:
multiple of 12 sts + 13; 12 rows

source: Haapsalu, handwritten

See page 123 for chart symbols.

Crown Prince Motif Variation

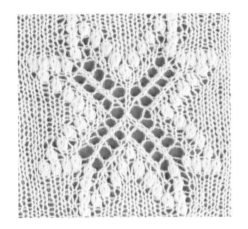

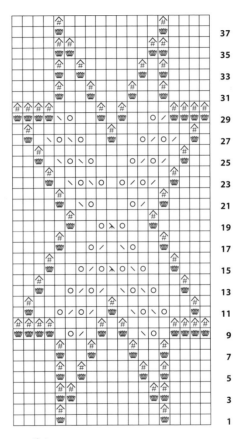

motif size:
19 sts and 38 rows

source: Haapsalu, handwritten

Greta Garbo Pattern 1

motif size:
17 sts and 34 rows

source: Haapsalu, handwritten

See page 123 for chart symbols.

Greta Garbo Pattern 2

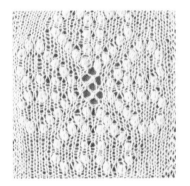

Greta Garbo Pattern 3

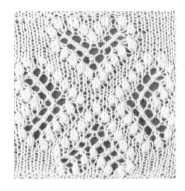

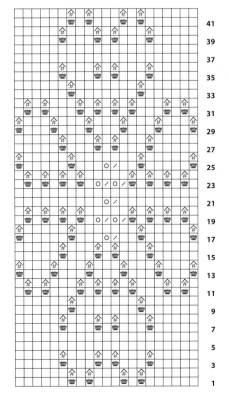

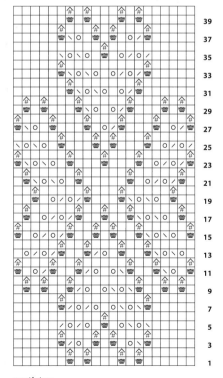

motif size:
21 sts and 42 rows

source: Haapsalu, handwritten

motif size:
21 sts and 40 rows

source: Haapsalu, handwritten

Edge Patterns

Äärepitsi Kiri (Lace Edge Pattern 1)

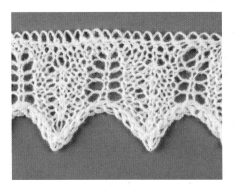

pattern repeat:
multiple of 10 sts + 11; 15 rows total

source: *Triinu* #8, 1955, in an article by Helve Poska

Cast on using a double strand of yarn. After RS Row 15, bind off on WS. This edge is best used knitted separately and then sewn around the sides of a rectangular or square shawl, or it can be used as the beginning and ending edge of a shawl without lacy edges, such as Madli's shawl.

Äärepitsi Kiri 2 (Lace Edge Pattern 2)

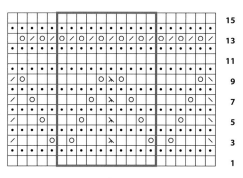

pattern repeat:
multiple of 10 sts + 11; 15 rows total

source: *Triinu* #87, 1974, in an article by Helve Poska

Cast on using a double strand of yarn. After RS Row 15, bind off on WS. This edge is best used knitted separately and then sewn around the sides of a rectangular or square shawl, or it can be used as the beginning and ending edge of a shawl without lacy edges, such as Madli's shawl.

See page 123 for chart symbols.

Äärepitsi Kiri 3 (Lace Edge Pattern 3)

pattern repeat:
multiple of 10 sts + 11; 15 rows total

source: *Triinu* #138, 1987, in an article by Salme Puus

Cast on using a double strand of yarn. After RS Row 15, bind off on WS. This edge is best used knitted separately and then sewn around the sides of a rectangular or square shawl, or it can be used as the beginning and ending edge of a shawl without lacy edges, such as Madli's shawl.

Äärepitsi Kiri 4 (Lace Edge Pattern 4)

pattern repeat:
multiple of 10 sts + 11; 15 rows total

source: *Triinu* #108, 1980, in an article by Salme Puus

Cast on using a double strand of yarn. After RS Row 15, bind off on WS. This edge is best used knitted separately and then sewn around the sides of a rectangular or square shawl, or it can be used as the beginning and ending edge of a shawl without lacy edges, such as Madli's shawl.

Äärepitsi Kiri 5 (Lace Edge Pattern 5)

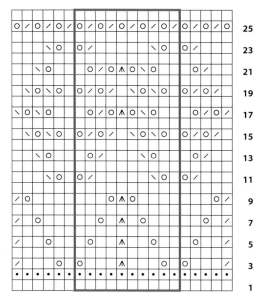

O	/	O	/	O	O	/	O	/	O	/	O	/	O	/	O	O	/	O	/	O	**25**
			\	O	O	/					\	O	O	/							**23**
		\	O			O	/	O	∧	O	\	O				O	/				**21**
	\	O	\	O	O	/	O	/		\	O	\	O	O	/	O	/				**19**
\	O	\	O			O	/	O	∧	O	\	O				O	/	O	/		**17**
	\	O	\	O	O	/	O	/		\	O	\	O	O	/	O	/				**15**
			\	O		O	/				\	O		O	/						**13**
		\	O	O	/				\	O	O	/									**11**
/	O					O	∧	O				O	/								**9**
/		O			O		∧		O			O		/							**7**
/			O		O		∧		O		O			/							**5**
/				O	O		∧			O	O			/							**3**
•	•	•	•	•	•	•	•	•	•	•	•	•	•	•	•	•	•	•	•	•	**1**

pattern repeat:
multiple of 10 sts + 11; 26 rows total

source: *Haapsalu Rätik*, New York, 1972

Cast on using a double strand of yarn.
This edge is best used at the top and bottom
of a rectangular shawl or as the edge.

See page 123 for chart symbols.

Äärepitsi Kiri 6 (Lace Edge Pattern 6)

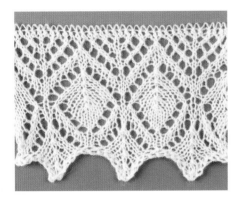

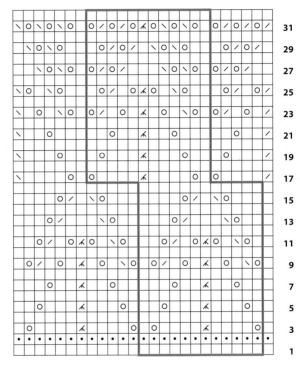

pattern repeat:
multiple of 12 sts + 13; 32 rows total

source: *Triinu* #106, 1979, in an article by Salme Puus

Cast on using a double strand of yarn. This edge is best used at the top and bottom of a rectangular shawl or as the edge of a triangular shawl, such as Miralda's Shawl.

Äärepitsi Kiri 7 (Lace Edge Pattern 7)

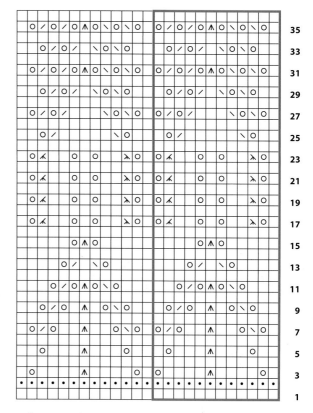

pattern repeat:
multiple of 12 sts + 1; 36 rows total

source: *Haapsalu Rätik*, New York, 1972

Cast on using a double strand of yarn. This edge is best used at the top and bottom of a rectangular shawl or as the edge of a triangular shawl, such as Miralda's Shawl.

See page 123 for chart symbols.

Äärepitsi Kiri 8 (Lace Edge Pattern 8)

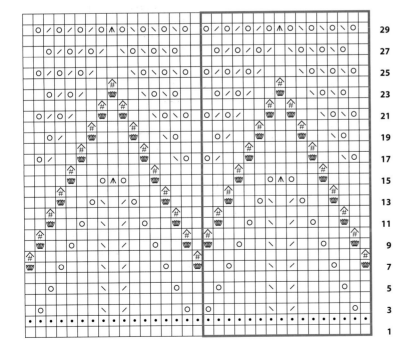

pattern repeat:
multiple of 16 sts + 1; 30 rows total

source: *Haapsalu Rätik*, New York, 1972

Cast on using a double strand of yarn.
This edge is best used at the top and
bottom of a rectangular shawl or as the edge
of a triangular shawl, such as Miralda's Shawl.

Modern 14-Round Lace Edge

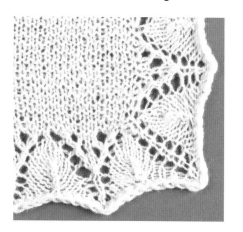

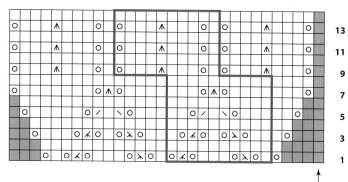

13
11
9
7
5
3
1

corner st

pattern repeat:
begins as a multiple of 10 sts + 1 and 1 corner st for each side;
14 rnds

source: Inspired by a knitted-on edge pattern
in Leili Reimann's *Pitsilised Koekirjad,* 1986 edition

Knit all even-numbered rounds as shown for a stockinette-stitch ground.
You may purl the even-numbered rounds for a garter-stitch ground,
although this is not as common in Estonia.

See page 123 for chart symbols.

Modern 16-Round Lace Edge

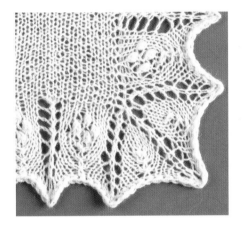

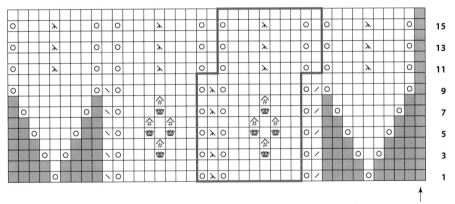

pattern repeat:
begins as a multiple of 10 sts + 1 and 1 corner st for each side;
16 rnds

source: From a shawl knitted by Hilja Aavik. It is also found in all three editions of
Leili Reimann's *Pitsilised Koekirjad*

All even-numbered rounds are knit as shown for a stockinette-stitch ground.
To complete the nupps on even-numbered rounds, knit all nupp stitches
together through their back loops.

Modern 24-Round Lace Edge

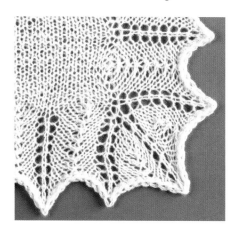

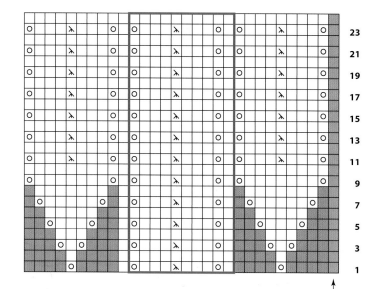

pattern repeat:
begins as a multiple of 10 sts + 1 and 1 corner st for each side; 24 rnds

source: From many shawls I have collected in Estonia,
from *Triinu* #116, 1982, in an article by Salme Puus, and also
found in all three editions of Leili Reimann's *Pitsilised Koekirjad*.

This knitted-on edge pattern is found on many shawls knitted in
Estonia today. The points are in line with the "k1, yo, k1" places
in the pattern, and this feature easily identifies knitted-on edges.
The bind-off for this type of edge is always worked using
the yarn doubled.

All even-numbered rounds are knitted as shown for a stockinette-stitch
ground. You may purl the even-numbered rounds for a garter-stitch
ground, although this is not as common in Estonia.

The number of rounds knitted depends on how deep you
want the edge to be. I recommend working at least 16 rounds
before the bind-off.

See page 123 for chart symbols.

BORDER PATTERNS

Border with Nupps

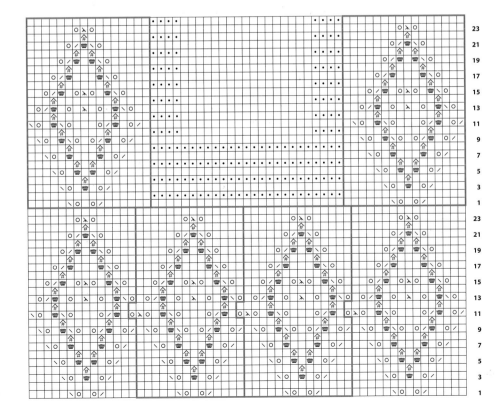

top and bottom
border motif:
multiple of 14 sts + 15;
24 rows
side motifs:
16 sts wide;
24 rows

source:
Haapsalu Rätik,
New York, 1972

This pattern is used
as an inner border for
a square shawl,
between the outer
garter edging and
the garter frame
around the center
section. The main
motif should be
worked the same
number of times
across the top and
bottom as along
each side.
See the Lehe
Square Shawl (page 56)
for an example.

Diamond Border

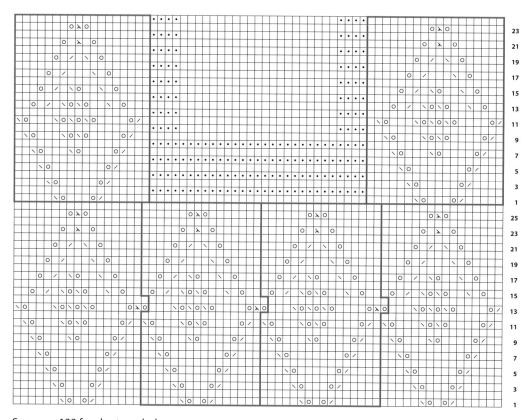

KNITTED LACE OF ESTONIA

top and bottom
border motif:
multiple of 16 sts + 17;
26 rows
side motifs:
18 sts wide;
24 rows

source:
Shawl in the
collection of the
Estonian National
Museum, Tartu, Estonia.

This pattern is used
as an inner border
for a square shawl,
between the outer
garter edging and
the garter frame
around the center
section. The main motif
should be worked the
same number of
times across the top
and bottom as along
each side. See the
Lehe Square Shawl (page 56)
for an example.

See page 123 for chart symbols.

ABBREVIATIONS

beg	begin(s); beginning		**rem**	remain(s); remaining
BO	bind off		**rep**	repeat(s); repeating
cm	centimeter(s)		**rnd(s)**	round(s)
CO	cast on		**RS**	right side
cont	continue(s); continuing		**sl**	slip
dec(s)	decrease(s); decreasing		**sl st**	slip st (slip 1 stitch purlwise unless otherwise indicated)
dpn	double-pointed needles		**st**	stitch(es)
foll	follow(s); following		**St st**	stockinette stitch
g	gram(s)		**tbl**	through back loop
inc(s)	increase(s); increasing		**tog**	together
k	knit		**WS**	wrong side
k1f&b	knit into the front and back of same stitch		**wyb**	with yarn in back
kwise	knitwise; as if to knit		**wyf**	with yarn in front
m	marker(s)		**yd**	yard(s)
mm	millimeter(s)		**yo**	yarnover
M1	make one (increase)		*****	repeat starting point
p	purl		**( )**	alternate measurements and/or instructions
p1f&b	purl into front and back of same stitch		**[ ]**	work instructions as a group a specified number of times
patt(s)	pattern(s)			
psso	pass slipped stitch over			
pwise	purlwise; as if to purl			

Sources for Yarns

**Aurora Yarns/
Omaghi Filati**
PO Box 3068, Moss Beach, CA 94038
aurorayarns.net

Habu Textiles
135 W. 29th St., Ste. 804, New York, NY 10001
habutextiles.com

Jamieson and Smith
90 North Rd., Lerwick, Shetland Islands
United Kingdom ZE1 0PQ
shetland-wool-brokers.zetnet.co.uk

Jojoland International
5615 Westwood Ln., The Colony, TX 75056
jojoland.com

Moco Yarns
301 Sandy Creek Rd., Tendoy, ID 83468
carylldesigns.com

Rovings
Box 28, Grp. 30, RR1, Dugald, MB
Canada R0E 0K0
rovings.com

Shelridge Farm
PO Box 1345, Durham, ON
Canada N0G 1R0
shelridge.com

Skacel
PO Box 88110, Seattle, WA 98138
skacelknitting.com

The Wooly West
PO Box 58306, Salt Lake City, UT 84158
woolywest.com

Yarn Place
3581 The Alameda, Santa Clara, CA 95050
yarnplace.com

Bibliography

Don, Sarah. *The Art of Shetland Lace.* Mills & Boon Limited, London, Sidney, Toronto, 1980.

Elgas, Linda. *Haapsalu Rätikud.* Haapsalu Käsitööselts, Haapsalu, 2001. Translation by Madli Puhvel.

Lehismets, Leili. *Pitsilised Koekirjad* (Knitted Lace). Valgus, Tallinn, 1978, first edition.
Reimann, Leili. *Pitsilised Koekirjad* (Knitted Lace). Valgus, Tallinn, 1986, second edition.
Reimann, Leili. *Pitsilised Koekirjad* (Knitted Lace). Monokkel, Tallinn, 1995, third edition.
Translations by Rita Tubalkain and Madli Puhvel.

Eesti Naisklubide Liit (Estonian Woman's Federation) *Haapsalu Rätik.* New York, 1972, editors: Helve Poska, Mari Loosme, Linda Pahk-Rõõmusmägi, and Frida Kaspar. Translation by Helena Soomer.

Fischer, Dorothea. *Maiglöckchen* (Lily of the Valley) Books on Demand. Norderstedt, 2004.
Translation by Gisela Chambers.

Hallik, Claire. *Silmus Kudumine.* Eesti Riiklik Kirjastus, Tallinn, 1957.

Khmeleva, Galina, and Carol Noble. *Gossamer Webs, The History and Techniques of Orenburg Lace Shawls.* Interweave, Loveland, Colorado, 1998.

Konsin, Kalju. Etnograafiamuuseumi *Aastaraamat XXII* (The Yearbook of the Ethnographic Museum XXII) Kirjastus Valgus. Tallinn, 1967.
Translation by Aire Salmre.

Miller, Sharon. *Heirloom Knitting, A Shetland Lace Knitter's Pattern and Workbook.* The Shetland Times Ltd. Lerwick, 2002.

Põldoja, Maimu. *Kudumine.* Valgus, Tallinn, 1992.

Stove, Margaret. *Creating Original Handknitted Lace.* Lacis Publications, Berkeley, California, 1998.

Triinu Magazine, published from 1952 to 1995, parts of many issues. Translations by Aire Salmre.

INDEX